Praise for Alan Dershowitz

"Alan Dershowitz, a principled man who takes the barbs better than anybody because he sticks to his principles and he doesn't really care whether you like him, and that's why he has fights with Larry David."
—**Megyn Kelly, host of *The Megyn Kelly Show***

"Perhaps the greatest lawyer in the world . . . a national treasure."
—**Gregg Kelly, TV host of *Greg Kelly Reports***

"A living profile in courage."

—**Steve Forbes**

"The fearless, peerless Alan Dershowitz."
—**Rabbi Lord Jonathan Sacks, late Chief Rabbi of Great Britain**

"Alan Dershowitz speaks with great passion and personal courage."
—**Elie Wiesel**

"An intellectual heavyweight."

—***The Economist***

"Astonishingly brilliant courtroom presence [and] a subtle and compelling theorist of civil liberties."
—**Henry Louis Gates**

"Loud, provocative, brilliant, and principled. . . ."

—**Politico**

"In fifty years of working with Alan Dershowitz, I have never met a more principled or honest advocate for truth."
—**Irwin Cotler, former Attorney General and Minister of Justice of Canada**

THE PRICE

of

PRINCIPLE

Why Integrity Is Worth the Consequences

ALAN DERSHOWITZ

Hot Books

Hot Books may be purchased in bulk at special discounts for sales promotion, corporate gifts, fund-raising, or educational purposes. Special editions can also be created to specifications. For details, contact the Special Sales Department, Skyhorse Publishing, 307 West 36th Street, 11th Floor, New York, NY 10018 or info@skyhorsepublishing.com.

Hot Books® and Skyhorse Publishing® are registered trademarks of Skyhorse Publishing, Inc.®, a Delaware corporation.

Visit our website at www.skyhorsepublishing.com.

10 9 8 7 6 5 4 3 2 1

Library of Congress Cataloging-in-Publication Data is available on file.

ISBN: 978-1-5107-7328-8
eBook: 978-1-5107-7329-5

Cover design by Brian Peterson

Printed in the United States of America

Acknowledgments

My wife, family, and friends have helped me live a life of principle and write about it.

Thanks to my assistant Maura Kelly, my editor Hector Carosso, my publisher Tony Lyons, and my friends Aaron Voloj, Alan Rothfeld, Marshall Sonenshine, and Harvey Silverglate for their constructive criticism.

And my appreciation to my friends—especially those who disagree with me—who have not abandoned me over our principled disagreements.

Dedication

At age eighty-three, the most important people in my life—aside from family and friends—are my doctors, who keep me able to write. This book is dedicated to them and to all doctors who serve humankind without sufficient appreciation.

Contents

Preface

This is my 50th book.[1]

I love writing. I write every day. I try to write 1,500–2,000 words a day (just as I try to walk five miles a day with my wife, and drink a glass of good wine with her, if I achieve my goals).

I have written about a wide array of subjects from criminal and constitutional law (my specialties) to the Bible, American history, Israel, moral philosophy, autobiography, politics, medicine, terrorism, sports, and delicatessen. I have written three novels and approximately 1,000 articles—law review scholarship, op-eds, magazine articles, and book reviews. I have been told that I have published <u>more</u>—not necessarily better—words than any Harvard professor in history. (I don't recall whether that was meant as a compliment.)

Descartes wrote "I think, therefore I am." For me, it is "I write, therefore I am." Recently I underwent surgery for the removal of my gallbladder that required general anesthesia. My doctor cautioned me that at age 83, the anesthesia might affect my cognitive abilities for a period of time. So as soon as I regained consciousness, I decided to write an op-ed to see whether my cognition was impaired. While

---

1 Four have been coauthored; 46 written by me alone.

in the recovery room, I typed an op-ed on my iPhone about the recent Supreme Court argument on abortion and submitted it. Its substance appears on pages 83 to 89 of this book. So you can judge whether I was compos mentis when I wrote it.

Nearly all of my writings are by hand. One year, my secretary estimated that she typed nearly a million of my handwritten words! I recently learned how to type short op-eds on my iPhone, and I dictate a bit. But handwriting is still my primary technique.

My handwritten drafts, which I generally preserve at least for a time, once protected me from a false charge of plagiarism. Norman Finkelstein, a virulent anti-Israel hater, tried to discredit my book, *The Case for Israel*, by claiming that I didn't write it—he said the Israeli Mossad ghosted it. When I produced my handwritten draft, he had to withdraw his absurd claim.

I hope to continue writing as long as I have the physical strength and mental capacity to do so. Eight of my books have been national bestsellers, including the *New York Times* #1 bestseller, *Chutzpah*. Two have been made into films. I'm proud of my writing, as I am of my teaching and litigating.

This book is about efforts to cancel me and my career, because I have insisted on sticking to my principles instead of choosing sides in the current culture and political war dividing our country. My opponents may succeed in temporarily cancelling me in certain venues and media, but they can never cancel my writing. The virtue of books—unless they are burned or permanently censored—is they endure beyond any particular era. Hence, my motivation to continue writing as I approach 84 years old.

How Partisanship Trumps Principle

W e live in an age in which partisanship has replaced principle as a dominant guide to actions, attitudes—even friendships. Today everyone must pick a side and support that side regardless of principles. In philosophy, this is known as the "NO true Scotsman fallacy." To be a "True Scotsman"—or true Democrat, progressive, Republican, American, Christian, Jew, African American, woman— one must adhere to <u>all</u> positions of the dominant ideology of the group, or else he or she ceases to be "true," "woke," "progressive," or "intersectional" in the current jargon. Adhering to principle is not accepted as an excuse for deviating from the groupthink on any issue. Everyone is put to a dichotomous choice: be "true" or be "false." (That is why in order to be a true progressive, one must be adamantly anti-Israel, even if one's personal principles might incline him to support at least some of Israel's policies and actions.) Being a true Scotsman means not picking or choosing based on principle but adhering to the entire agenda. There is no room for nuance or calibration. Neutral principles are not favored, unless they serve the ends of the group.

Few today care about passing the "shoe on the other foot" test for evaluating decisions: what would I do or think if the partisan roles were reversed? "Principles" have become just another weapon in the war of partisanship. Too many people today follow Groucho Marx's *bon mot*: "Those are my principles, and if you don't like them . . . well, I have others."

It is not as if the world was ever governed by principles alone, even at an earlier time. Free speech and due process "for me but not for thee" has been the rule rather than the exception for most people, but there have always been a significant number of people for whom principles matter. Today that number is shrinking—or being pressured to shrink—into oblivion. Genuinely principled, neutral people are an endangered species in our age of hyper partisanship.

Nor is this our first era of hyper partisanship. Although George Washington cautioned against divisive political parties, they have been with us since the end of Washington's second term. Adams, Jefferson, Hamilton, and Burr were only among the most visible dividers. The French Revolution, which Jefferson supported and Hamilton opposed, gave rise to the Alien and Sedition Acts, by which so called "Jacobins" were deported and/or prosecuted. Hamilton wrote, in words that may sound familiar to the current ear, of the favored weapons of the American Jacobins—namely "calumny":

A principal engine, by which this spirit endeavors to accomplish the purpose is that of calumny. It is essential to its success that the influence of men of upright principles, disposed and able to resist its enterprises, shall be at all events destroyed. Not content with traducing their best efforts for the public good, with misrepresenting their purest motives, with inferring criminality from actions innocent or landable, the most direct falsehoods are invented and propagated with undaunted effrontery and unrelenting perseverance. Lies often detected and refuted are still revived and repeated, in the hope that the refutation may have been forgotten, that the frequency and boldness of accusation may supply the truth and proof. The most profligate men are encouraged, probably bribed, certainly with patronage if not with money, to become informers and accusers. And when tales, which their characters alone ought to discredit, are refuted by the evidence and facts which oblige the patrons of them to abandon their support, they still continue in corroding whispers to wear away the reputations which they could not directly subvert.[1]

Little has changed in the two and a quarter centuries since these words were penned. Principles remain important only as <u>tools</u> of advocacy. Partisan advocacy masquerades as principled argument. Principles are stretched beyond all recognition in an effort to make it seem as if partisan arguments are grounded in principle. But only those who want to be fooled are fooled into believing that these arguments are truly motivated by principled considerations.

Advocates, especially lawyers, are trained to make partisan arguments <u>appear</u> principled, because they know that even in an age of partisanship, judges and others who evaluate arguments are more likely to be persuaded if they believe, or can claim to believe, the argument is grounded in neutral principles. Many judges and evaluators pretend to believe that the arguments they want to accept reflect principled positions, knowing full well that if the shoe were on the other foot, the advocate would be making precisely the opposite arguments.

It wasn't always this bad. Great philosophers, political theorists, and jurists grounded their arguments in neutrally applicable principles. Kant, Bentham, Spinoza, Mill, Rawls, Nozick, and others demanded that their principles—whether one agreed with them or not—be capable of neutral application. Indeed, many of them applied the shoe on the other foot test, though they used different words. John Rawls, most especially, set out a wide-ranging political philosophy that espoused the test most similar to the shoe on the other foot. He contemplated a nether world in which none of us knows whether we will be rich or poor, male or female, Black or

---

1   Alexander Hamilton, "Observations on certain documents contained in no. V & VI of 'The history of the United States for the year 1796,': in which the charge of speculation against Alexander Hamilton, late secretary of the Treasury, is fully refuted." 1797, 40.

white, Republican or Democrat, healthy or sick, intelligent or average, young or old. Blinded by this "veil of ignorance" we must articulate principles that would be maximally fair to <u>all</u> of us, without any of us knowing into which categories we would fit in the real world. So even if one wanted to act out of self or group interest, he could not, because he would not know what he would be or what group he would belong to when the time came to apply the principles.

Rawls is dead and tragically so are his principles. They are still solemnly cited by hypocritical academics who openly violate them in the interest of blatant partisanship, while pretending they are applying them neutrally.

When I was in law school, one of the most prominent professors, Herbert Wechsler, wrote an influential article entitled, "Toward Neutral Principles of Constitutional Law." Today, many academics would change it to, "Toward Partisan Principles of Constitutional Law"!

Many today, seem to care first and foremost about the identity of the people—that is why it is called "identity politics." Once they identify the objects of their advocacy, they construct so-called principles in order to advantage those whose identity they favor. Identity politics or jurisprudence, such as "critical race theory" (which is anything but critical about that propagandistic "theory") or "intersectionality" (which picks and chooses as to which groups are included) are precisely the opposite of "the veil of ignorance." Yet hypocritical academics cite the latter to justify the former. And naive students accept their professors' hypocrisy as the gospel truth, because their joint gospel is the so-called "progressive" or "woke" agenda, which elevates identity over principle.

Going back thousands of years, even the Bible demands of judges that they do not "recognize faces"—that they render justice behind a veil of ignorance regarding the identity of the litigants. That commandment—the rule against identity judging—precedes even the prohibition against accepting bribes. Yet today, faces come before fairness, identity before equality, and partisanship before principles.

Today, principled people are actively punished for not being sufficiently partisan. Principle has become the vice and partisanship the virtue in an age when partisan ends justify unprincipled means, such as denial of due process and free speech in the interest of achieving partisan or ideological goals. Fairness and equality have become microaggressions in an age where these time-tested principles have been equated with white privilege. University rules regard meritocracy as not only wrong but racist. In this topsy-turvy brave new world, it is a microaggression to say that "the most qualified person deserves the job"—except, of course, if one is undergoing surgery or flying in tempestuous weather, when any rational person would want their surgeon or pilot to be the most qualified.

In this short book, I will document this frightening devolution from principle to partisanship. I will argue that in an attempt to achieve a utopia of identify politics, we are on the road to a dystopia of partisanship and discrimination. I will name names and point fingers of accusation at those who have led us down this dangerous road. I will use my own experience as an advocate who insists on placing principle before partisanship, and I will document the attacks on me and others like me who are "guilty" of today's most heinous political offense: refusing to compromise important principles to promote partisanship.

In 1956, then Senator John Kennedy wrote a book entitled *Profiles in Courage*, which praised eight former senators who placed principle above partisanship and even above their own careers. Today, people still <u>say</u> they admire such principled courage, while at the same time punishing those who have displayed it, when it disadvantages the hypocrites who punish them. Courage "for me but not for thee" is the mantra in our current age of partisan divide.

David Brooks, writing in the *New York Times*, says that today we need "social courage" to cross "group lines and to have conversations," because "politics is no longer about argument; it's just jamming together a bunch of scary categories about people who are allegedly rotten to the core." Brooks notes, citing Professor Kwame Anthony Appiah, that contemporary politics is "almost all about identity—about which type of person is going to dominate."[2] This

---

2   Here's the mindset that is tearing us apart, October 7, 2021.

post–World War II emphasis on identity domination marks the death knell of principle as a motivating factor in decision making.

I will focus on three sets of principles that have dominated my life: 1) freedom of expression and conscience; 2) due process, fundamental fairness, and the adversary system of seeking justice; and 3) basic equality and meritocracy. I will consider other principles as well, but these three are central to any decent democracy and to the proper rule of law. I will subject all of my arguments to the shoe on the other foot test and stand behind only those that pass it.

The Bible commands "Justice, justice must you pursue," and the commentators ask why the word justice is repeated. Many answers have been given: procedural as well as substantive justice; justice to victim as well as accused; justice along with mercy. The one most appropriate to this book is that a rule or principle cannot be just for "me"; it must also be for "thee." True justice must be a two-way street. What is good for the goose must be good for the gander. Rabbi Hillel expounded on this concept when he summarized the Torah as setting out an early version of the golden rule: "What is hateful to you, do not do to your fellow-man." These are prescriptions for principled, rather than partisan, or identity justice. They are opposed to identity politics, critical race theory, and intersectionality.

When I was growing up, my grandmother—a refugee from the anti-Semitism of Poland—judged matters by her own variation of critical race theory. She would ask the same question about everything, ranging from the outcomes of elections to the results of baseball games: "Is it good or bad for the Jews?" Her parochial question—based on what can be denominated "uncritical Jew Theory"—was understandable in light of her history. And perhaps it is understandable for some African Americans, gays, women, and others who have experienced discrimination, to ask whether it is good or bad for their particular group, rather than for Americans in general or the world at large.

Justice Oliver Wendell Holmes taught us that "the life of the law has not been logic; it has been experience." As I demonstrated in my 2005 book, *Rights from Wrongs*, experience is more than the life of the law; it is the basis of all human rights. Philosophy is often autobiography. But experiences are not static. They change over time, for individuals as well as for groups. While this self-serving question—is it good for my group?—might be understandable at some stage in a group's evolution, it is not the right question for a society consisting of multiple, overlapping racial, religious, ethnic, gender, sexual orientation, political, ideological, and other groups. What is good for any particular group may not be good policy for an entire nation.

In a democracy, the needs and preferences of every group must be taken into account and then balanced against the needs and preferences of all other groups and individuals. A fair and effective democracy must have processes and procedures for balancing these factors and arriving at a just resolution. No group should have a veto. Nor should any group be ignored. The rules for resolving contentious and divisive issues must be systemically fair, favoring or disfavoring no group or individual. And fairness requires neutral principles, not identity or partisan preferences. This is the challenge of a democracy governed by the rule of law.

The thesis of this book is that we are not meeting this challenge. To the contrary, we are punishing principle and rewarding unprincipled partisanship and identity politics. We are discouraging young people from living lives of principle, by cancelling, ostracizing, and condemning those who place principle over result-oriented partisanship. We are teaching students by example that they will be better off being politically correct than principally consistent. They see how those who refuse to pick sides are treated as pariahs, while those who are prepared to sacrifice principle on the altar of partisanship are rewarded.

As a law professor and defense lawyer for nearly 60 years, I am particularly concerned about the impact this punishment of principle is having on those contemplating careers in the law or politics. Since a young John Adams defended the hated British soldiers who were accused of killing American patriots in what became known as the "Boston Massacre," principled criminal defense lawyers have defended hated individuals with whose actions they personally disagree. This honorable tradition was followed by the likes of Daniel Webster, Abraham Lincoln, Clarence Darrow, Thurgood Marshall, Edward Bennett Williams, and many other brave lawyers whose names are not remembered by history. Some were praised for supporting the constitutional right to counsel. Others were condemned. Many went on to distinguished careers at the bar and in politics. Others were forgotten. Never before—with the exception of McCarthyism about which I will write shortly—have such principled lawyers been punished to the degree they have been recently.

I will describe these punishments in detail in forthcoming chapters, including recent attacks by some Republican senators against judicial nominees who had served as public defenders. It is enough to say here, in this introduction, that many law students and young lawyers have told me and others that they will never become defense lawyers, having witnessed the personal and professional attacks on me and others who have put principle before partisanship. My own research assistant told me that he completely agreed with my Senate defense of President Trump against unconstitutional impeachment charges, but that he could not assist me for fear that his participation would result in his being blackballed for future jobs. Others have told me of similar concerns. They are not wrong, as a matter of fact. This is both a tragedy and a danger to the rule of law.

Among the precipitating causes of this divisive shift was the election and incumbency of Donald Trump. Many on the left, and even some in the center, regarded him as such an existential threat to their values that anyone who helped him in any way was damned as an enabler, even if their actions were based on longstanding constitutional principles. It was similar to what I remember as a student when international communism was seen by many on the right, and some in the center, as an existential threat to the American way of life. The Soviet Union had seized control of much of Eastern and Central Europe. Cuba and China were ruled by communists. Nikita Khrushchev threatened to "bury" America. In the United States, communists and former communists were alleged to be in positions of authority in sensitive governmental jobs. Many were thought to be in academia and the entertainment industry. Regardless of whether this fear was exaggerated—I think it was—it was widely believed.

Many Americans in the 1950s were as frightened of communism as many on the left and in the center were fearful of Trump in the recent past—and even now.

Anyone who was seen as assisting communism in any way was condemned as a "fellow traveler." They were persecuted, ostracized and worse, even if they acted on principle as many anti-communists civil libertarian lawyers did.

There was—and is—a similar reaction to Trumpism. Principle is among the first casualties of fear. It is regarded as an unaffordable luxury at a time when results are needed. And the result that was most needed by those who were frightened was the defeat of Trump and his policies by any means, regardless of principle or process. And anyone who stood in the way of that essential result—whether on the basis of principle or partisanship—was regarded as a Trump enabler, supporter and water carrier, even if he or she voted against him and strongly supported his opponents. The same had been true of anti-communists who defended the civil liberties and constitutional rights of communists against McCarthyism. The difference is that the old McCarthyism was directed by the right against left-wing and centrist civil libertarians. Whereas the new McCarthyism is directed by the left against anyone who dares to defend the constitutional rights of Trump and his allies. The victims of both iterations of McCarthyism are the same: Civil libertarians who place principle above partisanship. I know, because I'm one of these "victims," and as I will show, I'm paying a high price for acting on principles. But I am fighting back. I refuse to accept victimhood for doing the right thing. I am fighting both to defend my own integrity and to encourage young women and men to live principled lives, to resist the slings and arrows that have been directed at me and others, and to continue in the noble tradition of Adams, Lincoln, Darrow, and Marshall by zealously defending the constitutional rights of the despised, the guilty, the dangerous, and even the political pariahs.

I write about myself because I am among the most high-profile defense lawyers who have been attacked—cancelled—for my defense of the Constitution on behalf of former President Trump and others. *New York* magazine characterized me as "his generation's answer

to Clarence Darrow, the legendary 'attorney for the damned.'"
I hope I can live up to that compliment. I have been called—for
better or worse—"the best known criminal lawyer in the world."
Accordingly, if the attack on me succeeds, it will have an exponen-
tiary impact on young people considering careers similar to mine.
"I don't want to be 'Dershowitzed,'" one law student told me. But
if "being Dershowitzed" means being punished for placing principle before partisanship, I want young people to be proud of "being
Dershowitzed" and to fight back against such punishment.

In the chapters to come, I will elaborate on the important principles that are at stake in the attacks on me and others; how these
principles are being subordinated to partisan and identity politics;
and why dialogue, debate, and open-mindedness have been replaced
by ad hominem bumper stickers. I will point out the main culprits in
this attack on principles and provide numerous examples of this new
brand of McCarthyism at work. Finally, I will warn about the broad
implications of punishing principle and rewarding partisanship and
try to answer the most difficult question of all: can we reverse this
dangerous trend, or are we destined to live for the foreseeable future
in a divided world in which partisanship trumps principle?

Hence this book.

CHAPTER I

The Important Principles for Which I Am Willing to Pay a Heavy Price

From the time I was a teenager, I have lived by certain principles that haven't changed much over the past nearly 70 years. Central among them are the freedom of speech and expression for all; due process and equal protection of the laws; and the right of every accused person to a zealous legal defense.

Although I have always been a liberal Democrat, I have never put party over principle. Even my critics have acknowledged—sometimes grudgingly—that I live by my principles. (*Politico*, in a somewhat critical article, described me as "loud, provocative, brilliant, and principled.") Nor have I limited freedom of speech only to expressions with which I agree; neither have I limited due process and the defense of the accused to innocent or good people. To the contrary, I have gone out of my way to be sure that these principles must be applied equally to people I despise, to ideas I oppose, and to the party against which I regularly vote. The ideological shoe must comfortably fit on the other foot. As H. L. Mencken once put it: "The trouble with fighting for human freedom is that one spends most of one's time defending scoundrels. For it is against scoundrels that oppressive laws are first aimed, and oppression must be stopped at the beginning if it is to be stopped at all." I have spent much of my life defending bad people, bad speech, and bad acts in an effort to combat bad laws.

In theory many, perhaps even most, citizens probably agree with the equal application of these principles, without regard to party or person. But in practice, they tend to apply them selectively to chosen parties, persons, and other identity preferences. Too many people not only "recognize faces," as the Bible prohibits, they place identity over neutral principles. They admire and praise defenders of civil liberties when these liberties facilitate and enable policies they favor, people they like, and parties they support. But they despise and condemn these same defenders when these same principles facilitate and enable their political enemies.

The problem with such a selective approach is that civil liberties—freedom of expression, due process, equal protection, zealous representation—only work when they are applied to all. If they are applied selectively, today they may favor the left, tomorrow the right, and soon no one. Liberty for me but not for thee endangers liberty for all, since the "me" and "thee" inevitably change. As Pastor Martin Niemöller reminded us shortly after the Holocaust:

> First they came for the socialists, and I did not speak out—because I was not a socialist.
>
> Then they came for the trade unionists, and I did not speak out—because I was not a trade unionist.
>
> Then they came for the Jews, and I did not speak out—because I was not a Jew.
>
> Then they came for me—and there was no one left to speak for me.

Niemöller's statement is well known. What is not well known is the reason he did not speak out for the Jews: he was, as he later acknowledged, an anti-Semite. He learned the painful lesson that failure to defend the rights of the "thee"—even the thee you despise—will eventually cause the denial of the rights for the "me."

Having grown up in the immediate aftermath of the Holocaust, I have always spoken out for, and defended the rights of the "thee"—of causes and people I disagree with, such as communists, Nazis, anti-Semites, anti-Zionists, right wingers, criminals, corrupt politicians, and other "bad people." I have also defended good causes and good people. I support the Constitution, not necessarily those individuals who invoke it for their own benefit. As a result, I am praised by those who favor my clients and condemned by those who disfavor them. The end result is that I am condemned more often than praised, because I pride myself on being called "the lawyer of last resort"—the one they come to when no one else will take their case. And clients of "last resort" most often turn out to be widely despised, with few supporters or friends—not always but often enough. I have chosen this career and I understand the price I must pay for my choice.

But to understand is not to condone. It is wrong to selectively praise and condemn civil libertarians based on the clients and causes that happen to be invoking the liberty at issue. If one opposes civil liberties in general—as some do—then it is consistent to criticize those who defend them for anyone. Just as it is consistent for those who support civil liberties to praise those who defend them for all. What is inconsistent, though widely practiced, is to <u>support</u> civil liberties, and yet to <u>condemn</u> those who defend them for all, including those you disagree with (see Chapter 10). That is not civil liberties as a neutral principle, but rather as a partisan tactic.

A. Free Speech for All

Today for the first time in my memory, mainstream academics and politicians are expressly denouncing the concept of free speech for all. They argue that the freedom to express negative views about disadvantaged people and progressive causes is patriarchal, colonialist—even white supremacist. They would reserve freedom of speech for those who they claim have been silenced throughout history. They would deny constitutional protection to hate speech, while defining hate speech as directed only to certain preferred identities. They claim that the marketplace of ideas is as distorted as the marketplace of other products, favoring the privileged over the unprivileged. This fear of free speech was manifested by the progressive reaction to Elon Musk's purchase of Twitter and the concern that—in the words of NAACP president Derrick Johnson—he would allow "unacceptable

. . . disinformation, misinformation, and hate speech"—as if those were objective and self-defining terms.

Throughout history there have been those who have sought to limit freedom of speech to only certain groups or individuals. Communists limited speech to supporters of communism. McCarthyites limited speech to opponents of communism. Some religious leaders denied freedom of expression to disbelievers, heretics, and skeptics. All of these censors had justifications for the limitations they would impose. Today, according to a *New York Times* poll, it is "Democrats and liberals [who] showed a higher level of support for sometimes shutting down speech [that is] anti-democratic, bigoted, or simply untrue."[1] America has a free speech problem. In March of 2022, more than 100 Yale Law School students tried to disrupt speakers who were seen as anti-gay, and more than 11,000 people sought to cancel an opera about the murder of Emmett Till because it was written by a white woman. There are many more examples of "woke" censorship.

Once, in a class I asked the students for a show of hands on whether they support free speech for ideas they oppose. Every hand went up. I asked who would make an exception for claims that Blacks are racially inferior? Several hands went up. I then asked how may would make an exception for Holocaust denial? A few more hands. For pornographic films glorifying rape? A few more. For claims that homosexual conduct is immoral? Several more. By the time I had finished cataloguing all plausible exceptions, it became obvious that if any one group got to censor its most disfavored genre of speech, then every other group would demand equal power to censor its most disfavored genre, and that the exceptions would swallow the rule. The one conclusion that seems clear is that the government should not be permitted to pick and choose among speech that deeply offends some, but not others. Offensiveness is in the eye—and the history—of the beholder.

The reality, demonstrated by history, is that there are only two possibilities when it comes to freedom of speech: (1) a regime of

---

1   Editorial Board, "America Has a Free Speech Problem," *New York Times*, March 18, 2022.

selective censorship, in which only certain kinds of speech is permitted, depending on those making the decision; or (2) complete freedom of speech for all, limited only by neutral, non-content-based restrictions, such as time, place, and manner limitations. No system of restricting speech has ever succeeded in striking an appropriate balance between neutral freedom of expression and preventing speech that is deemed undesirable by some. The appetite of the censor is veracious. Once given the power to suppress <u>undesirable</u> speech, the pressure to suppress <u>more</u> becomes irresistible. Every offended group demands equality of treatment: namely that material they deem offensive also be banned in the name of equity.

The choice is between what I call "the taxicab theory of free speech" and a "system of censorship." Just as a taxicab must accept all law-abiding passengers who can pay the fare, without discriminating on the basis of where they were going or why they are going there, so too a government or a university should not pick and choose between what speeches, books, or magazines may be offensive. Once it gets into the business of picking and choosing among viewpoints, then it must create a fair and equitable system of censorship based on articulated principles. If it decides that items offensive to some women can be banned, then it will have difficulty rejecting the claims of offensiveness made by African Americans, Jews, gays, fundamentalist Christians, atheists, vegetarians, anti-fur proponents, and other politically correct and incorrect groups. I call this "-ism equity."

Both alternatives—pervasive censorship and -ism equity—produce less freedom of expression. The social media are facing precisely this dilemma now. In addition to demands for equal treatment, any institution that edits selectively on the basis of the alleged <u>falsity</u> of the censored material faces the following conundrum: if Facebook, Twitter, and You Tube take down content which they deem to be <u>untrue</u>, then at least some viewers may come to believe that content that is <u>not</u> taken down must have passed the test of *truthfulness*. That is surely misleading at best, since the vast majority of untrue content is not taken down. So, when social media get into the business of selectively censoring some untruths, it is *they* who may be promoting the false belief in the alleged truth of the untruths they do not censor. It is a no-win situation.

Under a system of censorship—whose paradigm was the former Soviet Union—the state must literally approve everything that is officially published (hence the term samizdat—illegally self-published without approval of the state). Everything that is published reflects affirmative government policy. Everything that is turned down for publication is against governmental policy. There are no neutral publications that are neither approved nor disapproved by the state but merely tolerated. There are no gray zones. No Soviet high official was ever heard to paraphrase Voltaire by saying to an author, "I disagree with what you are saying but I will defend your right to say it." China and Iran are today's paradigms of government control of speech.

The neutral model is one that no nation in history has ever achieved. But ours comes closest to it, at least at times. The model is one of content neutrality. The state neither approves nor disapproves of what is published in newspapers, magazines, TV, or the internet. Indeed it does not even learn what is being published until after it has hit the streets or the internet (hence the importance of the prohibition against prior restraint). When an offensive item is published, the government can—and should—disclaim all responsibility for its content. The content simply put, is none of the government's business. The government (or the university or internet platform) has neither approved it nor disapproved it.

Once the government gets into the business of disapproving of content on grounds of offensiveness it has lost its claim to neutrality, and the trouble begins.

Assume that a group of militant feminists argues to a local government that a particular pornographic film—say, Deep Throat, which I defended—is so offensive to women that it should be banned. Officials view the film, agree with the feminists, and ban it from their city. The next week, a group of Blacks argues that the film Birth of a Nation is at least as offensive to Blacks as Deep Throat is to women; a group of Jews will argue that the Nazi films of Leni Riefenstahl are as offensive as *Birth of a Nation* and *Deep Throat*; a group of gays will make the same claim about the film *Cruising*.

If there is one thing that is clear about offensiveness, it is that there is no objective basis for comparison. If obscenity is in the eye of the beholder—or, as Justice William O. Douglas once quipped, "in the crotch of the beholder"—then offensiveness lies deep in the history and psyche of those who feel it. Can anyone—especially a government—make any comparative assessment of the offensiveness felt by a concentration camp survivor seeing a swastika, a descendant of a slave seeing a burning cross, a woman who has been raped seeing a positive portrayal of sexual brutalization? If the government is to ban one, it must ban all. If it is to refuse to ban any, it must refuse to ban all.

A story from my own experience illustrates this conundrum. I once represented Soviet dissidents at a Helsinki Human Rights conference. During a meeting with Soviet officials, I complained about the recent publication of certain blatantly anti-Semitic material. The official responded—quite expectedly—by telling me that worse materials were published in the United States. I agreed and took out copies of some horrible anti-Semitic material published here and showed them to him. I also showed him some of the copies of the material published in the Soviet Union. I asked him to look at both and tell me the difference. He understood immediately. The Soviet material bore a stamp signifying that it had been approved by Glavlit, the official censorship agency of the Soviet Union. The American material had been approved by no one except the National Socialist White People's party—whose stamp it bore. The Soviet material was awful; the American material was worse. But the Soviet material carried the imprimatur of its government—a government that will not allow the publication of material deemed offensive by favored groups but will encourage the publication of material deemed offensive to disfavored groups. Therein lies the difference—and a critical difference it is.

I have been fighting for maximum freedom of speech during my entire lifetime.

The struggle has never been greater than now, because those advocating restrictions of free speech are often on the right side of other issues. Even the American Civil Liberties Union has begun to compromise its support for free speech. It now demands that a balance must be struck between freedom of speech and the quest for equality, as defined by its largely left-wing members. The ACLU is no longer the neutral defender of all free speech that it once was.

The enemy of freedom of speech and due process has always been "certainty" and "dogma." Those who are certain about the correctness of their views and the incorrectness of contradictory ones see no need for dissent or the open marketplace of ideas or due process.

Those who censor in the name of ideology, religion, even scientific certainty often fail to understand the need to have their views challenged. As the great Judge Learned Hand said:

"The spirit of liberty is the spirit which is not too sure that it is right; the spirit of liberty is the spirit which seeks to understand the mind of other men and women; the spirit of liberty is the spirit which weighs their interests alongside its own without bias." By these standards, the spirit of liberty is in grave danger in our universities, in the media, and in other walks of Amerian life.

Certainty and dogma have also long been the enemy of due process and the right to a zealous defense.

B. Due Process and the Right of Zealous Representation

For those who are certain about the appropriate outcome of cases, due process and the right to zealous representation are simply barriers to the truth. A current example will make the point. Many radical feminists are certain that women never lie or make mistakes with regard to rape or sexual assault. When I was invited to give a lecture at Colgate University, a group of radical feminists protested on the grounds that I am "an accused child rapist." A woman who I had never met falsely accused me of having sex with her when she was above the age of consent. I disproved her accusation by documentary records and the admission of her own lawyers. (See my book, *Guilt by Accusation the Challenge of Proving Innocence in the Age of #MeToo*, which contains all the relevant documentary evidence, summarized here in Chapter 2.) My false accuser eventually withdrew the allegation from a lawsuit we each brought. But none of this mattered to these extremists who believe that women always tell the truth. For them, there is no need for due process, legal representation, or even a trial. This is what the Colgate group wrote: "Considering only 2.1% of rape accusations are false, should we be welcoming him to campus." First of all, that statistic is categorically false: rape actually has among the highest percentage of false charges of any felony—well over 2 percent, according to Justice Department statistics. But even if their made up statistic were true, it wouldn't prove MY alleged guilt. The vast majority of rape accusations are against men who acknowledge they knew the women, and many are against men who also admit having sex with them, claiming it was consensual. I proved conclusively I never met her. But these radicals are certain I must be guilty because I'm an accused man, and they are not interested in hearing any evidence that might shake their ideological certainty and dogma.

Justice Felix Frankfurter once aptly observed that the history of liberty is largely a history of procedure—of due process, right to counsel, the presumption of innocence, and other liberty truth-protecting mechanisms that the radical left is out to destroy in the name of certainty. The history of liberty is also a history of free speech, which is being targeted by those who place partisanship, ideology, and certainty above the search for truth and the liberty to pursue it. And the history of liberty includes the quest for equality, rather than advantages or disadvantages based on race, sex, religion, or other such identities.

C. Equal Protection of the Law and Meritocracy

I have just written a book on this issue entitled *The Case for Color Blind Equality in an Age of Identity Politics*. I argue for the principle of meritocracy and equality that Martin Luther King dreamt for: a time when individuals are judged not by the color of their skin but by the quality of their character and other relevant criteria. I have always lived by that principle. Indeed, even early in my career I risked tenure by opposing discrimination.

Shortly after I was appointed to the Harvard Law School faculty, I received a call from Judge Bailey Aldrich inviting me to present a talk to the members of his private club, called the "Club of Odd

Volumes." He assured me that its members included some of the best and most important lawyers in Boston, including several justices of the Supreme Court and other judges. They would invite all the "new dons to tell us about their work," he advised me.

I told Judge Aldrich that I would get back to him. I then called the head of the Anti-Defamation League and inquired about the club. "They don't accept Jews, Catholics, Blacks, or women," he responded. I called Judge Aldrich and told him that I had a strict policy against speaking at any "restricted" club and so I would respectfully have to decline his kind invitation. (I adopted that "policy" that day, having never before been invited to speak at a restricted, or any other, club.) He thanked me for considering the invitation. Within an hour, I was abruptly summoned to the dean's office.

Dean Irwin Griswold informed me that I had offended one of the law school's most important alumni, that I was the only assistant professor ever to turn down an invitation to speak at that club, and that it was important for untenured faculty to present their work there, because several of the members served on the Harvard Board of Overseers, which approved all the tenured decisions. He chided me: "You've hurt your chances. Why did you decline their invitation? Will you reconsider it if I can get them to invite you again?"

I said no and explained my reasons. Griswold paused, looked directly at me, and said, "While I don't agree with you, considering your background I can understand why you would feel uncomfortable at the club. I'll call Bailey and try to explain. I hope you haven't hurt your chances." That was the last I heard, until a few years later, when Dean Griswold informed me that the chairman of the overseers subcommittee being asked to review and approve the faculty decision recommending me for tenure was an active member of "the club." I was ready for a fight. But I was approved, the dean later told me, by unanimous vote.

Several years after I began teaching, I was invited to deliver a named lectureship at a major university. Following my talk, there was a dinner at the local university club. When I got to the club, several women were picketing because it was a men's-only club. I refused to cross the picket line, and the dinner had to be moved to a different venue, over the strong objections of the chief justice of the state, who had sponsored the dinner.

Several years later, I was invited to Australia to give a series of lectures, and the Harvard Club of Sydney asked me to give a luncheon talk. I agreed. When I mentioned to a friend that I was going to be speaking at the Australia club, he advised me that it was closed to Jews, women, and Blacks. I gave the club two options: I would keep my commitment, but I would speak about why it was wrong for Harvard to hold events at segregated clubs, or they could move the speech and I would give a talk about life at Harvard. They chose the second alternative. When I returned to Harvard, I wrote to the dean, and a memo was circulated mandating that henceforth no Harvard professors, speaking on behalf of Harvard, should appear in a segregated venue. When a Jewish country club in Boston asked me to talk, I declined the invitation. They explained that the club had been established in reaction to the unwillingness of other country clubs in the area to accept Jewish members. I told them that this did not justify further discrimination. The membership chairman called and told me that, in fact, the club had six non-Jewish members. I made the speech. A young member approached me and told me I had been conned: "Sure, we have six non-Jewish members, but they're all sons-in-law of Jewish members."

Throughout my life, I have lived by the principle of non-discrimination, even in favor of Jews. "Equality for me but not for thee," does not satisfy the "shoe on the other foot" test.

D. The Right to Zealous Defense for All: or Why I Defend the Guilty and Innocent Alike

Sometimes it takes personal encounters to understand why it is so important for lawyers to defend even very bad people.

Several weeks after the verdict in the O. J. Simpson double murder case, my wife Carolyn and I were walking down Madison Avenue in New York when a well-dressed woman approached us and said, "I used to love you so much, and now I'm so disappointed in you—and my husband would use even stronger words." She explained, "You used to defend Jews like Sharansky and Pollard. Now you defend a Jew-killer like O. J." I replied that she was wrong ever to have loved me because she probably didn't understand what I do. A few blocks further along, a Black man hugged me and said, "Great job. I love what you do." I told him not to love what I do or else he would soon be disappointed.

A few years after that, my wife was involved in a minor litigation. The controversy was sent to mediation where both sides were represented by excellent lawyers. The lawyer for the opposing side was anxious to settle the matter, since my wife was clearly in the right both legally and morally. (We agreed to mediation only because litigation, which we would have won, would have been incredibly time-consuming and expensive.) I was at the mediation to lend support to my wife, who is a psychologist, not a lawyer. The opposing lawyer was, in my view, particularly nice and extremely polite, but he represented his client—a particularly sleazy enterprise—with vigor. At the first recess my wife, who rarely has a negative word to say about anyone, was furious at the opposing lawyer. With a wry irony, she fumed, "How can he represent these people? Doesn't he know he's on the wrong side? How does he sleep at night?"

My wife smiled at me, acknowledging that she was saying all of the same things that people say about me when I represent clients they believe are guilty, bad, or wrong. Only after she won the case and got a nice settlement did she really calm down. "I guess I'm equating him with his client," my wife said sheepishly. "That's what they always do to you."

Imagine a legal system in which lawyers were equated with the clients they defended and were condemned for representing controversial or despised defendants. Actually, one need not resort to imagination, since history reminds us that only a little more than half a century ago, mainstream lawyers were frightened away from defending alleged communists who faced congressional witch hunts, backlisting, criminal trials, and even execution (the Rosenbergs). Senator Joseph McCarthy and the millions of Americans—including many lawyers, law professors, and bar association leaders—who supported this attack on "commie-symp lawyers" made it impossible for decent lawyers who despised communism but who supported civil liberties and constitutional rights for all to defend accused communists without risking their careers.

I grew up at a time when Julius and Ethel Rosenberg were accused of being Soviet spies who gave the secret of the atomic bomb to our archenemies. They were defended by a communist ideologue with little experience in criminal cases. He provided an inept defense resulting in a terrible miscarriage of justice that has only recently been confirmed by Soviet intelligence sources. It now seems clear that the government framed Ethel Rosenberg in a futile effort to get her husband, who was a minor spy, to disclose the names of his accomplices who were major spies There is no assurance that an able and zealous mainstream lawyer could have saved either or both Rosenbergs from the electric chair, but we should certainly be left with an uncomfortable feeling that McCarthyite attacks on lawyers may well have contributed to a terrible injustice—and some very bad law—in the Rosenberg and other cases during the late 1940s and 1950s.

Even one of my favorite books—*To Kill a Mockingbird*—portrays America's most popular fictional character, Atticus Finch, as representing an apparently guilty Black defendant who, in the end turns out to be completely innocent. One must wonder whether the novel would have been as successful, or its hero as admired, if the accused turned out to be guilty. My other fictional hero, Perry Mason, not only proved all his clients innocent but also fingered the guilty killer so that perfect justice could be done.

In many parts of the real world, it remains difficult for a despised defendant to be represented by a mainstream lawyer because many, even Western-style democracies, lack any tradition of a political or civil libertarian representation. For example, in Israel, which has an excellent legal system, right-wing lawyers tend to represent right-wing defendants (especially "settlers" on the West Bank), while left-wing lawyers tend to represent left-wingers and Palestinians accused of political crimes. (The situation in Israel has improved somewhat in recent years, thanks to a developing legal aid system, while the situation in the United States has gotten worse.) This ideological approach to legal representation creates a circular reality in which lawyers are expected to share the political perspectives of their clients. The result is a bar divided along ideological lines that lack a neutral commitment to civil liberties for all. A similar situation prevails in France, Italy, and some other European countries.

Our nation had long been blessed with the tradition of a vigorous bar committed to civil liberties for all, regardless of ideology, politics, or the nature of the accusation. It would be a terrible tragedy if we were to surrender this noble tradition to those who are so certain about their ability to discover truth that they become impatient with the often imperfect process of justice. Remember Judge Learned Hand: "the spirit of liberty is the spirit that is not too sure that it is right."

It is a rare case in which absolute truth resides clearly on one side. Most cases contain shades of gray and are matters of degree. That has surely been true of most of the cases in which I have participated over my career. Even in those that are black and white, either the defendant did it or he did not—there is often room for disagreement, and it is the advocates' role to present the client's perspective zealously within the bounds of law and ethics. Zealous representation requires the lawyer to subordinate all other interests—ideological, career, personal—to the legitimate interest of the client. You are the surgeon in the operating room whose only goal is to save the patient whether that patient is a good person or a bad person, a saint or a criminal. It is a rare case in which a lawyer knows for sure that his client is guilty and that there are no mitigating considerations. In most of those cases, the lawyer will try to persuade the defendant to enter into a plea bargain—not because that is best for society or the legal system, but because it is best for the client.

Having made this general point, it is important to suggest several distinctions among types of legal representation. At the pinnacle of cases that should be defended vigorously without regard to ideology are criminal charges, free speech, and other constitutional protections. Surely those of us who defend free speech rights of everyone—including extremists on the right and left, purveyors of sexual material, and newspapers that make honest mistakes—should not be deemed to approve of the content of the materials the government seeks to censor. Those of us who opposed efforts by the town of Skokie to censor Nazis did not sympathize with the Nazis. We opposed censorship even of the most despicable and false ideas. It should be equally obvious that those who chose to defend people facing execution or long imprisonment do not sympathize with murder, rape, robbery, or corporate crime. I personally despise criminals and always root for the good guys except when I am representing one of the bad guys. We believe in the process of American justice, which requires zealous advocacy, scrupulous compliance with constitutional safeguards, and the rule of law. We understand that most people brought to trial for serious crimes are factually guilty. Thank goodness for that!

Would anyone want to live in a country in which the majority of criminal defendants were innocent? This may be true of China, Cuba, Belarus, Iran, and Syria, but it is certainly not true of the United States. And in order to keep it that way, every defendant—regardless of his or her probability of guilt, unpopularity, or poverty—must be vigorously defended within the rules of ethics. If lawyers were to defend only accused criminals whom they believed were innocent, more actually innocent defendants would be convicted. It is also true that fewer actually guilty defendants would be acquitted. But if we truly believe that it is better for ten guilty defendants to be acquitted than for one innocent to be convicted, then this trade-off is essential.

The scandal is not that the rich are zealously defended; it is that the poor and middle class are not. More resources should be allocated to defending those who cannot afford to challenge the prosecution and to expose the weaknesses of the evidence against them.

There are indeed some innocent people in prison and on death row, and it is no coincidence that most of them are poor and unable to secure effective legal advocacy. That is why I devote half of my time to pro bono cases. Many other lawyers also do a significant amount of free legal representation, but this is not enough to ensure that no defendant faces execution or long imprisonment without zealous advocacy on his behalf. If lawyers are frightened away from taking on unpopular criminal cases, the already serious problem of inadequate representation will reach crisis proportions. There is no surer way of frightening a young lawyer who is contemplating the defense of an accused murdered or rapist than to accuse him or her of being sympathetic to murder or sexual abuse.

Of course, a lawyer has the legal and ethical option of declining to represent an unpopular and despised defendant whom he believes to be guilty. The real question is whether it is desirable for the decent lawyer to exercise that option on the basis of the "politically correct" criterion of the day, which differs over time. Today, it is popular to represent communists because communism presents no threat, but it is unpopular to represent Islamic fundamentalists accused of terrorism, right-wing extremists accused of racist crimes, well-known men charged with sex crimes or despised politicians such as Donald Trump. I believe no lawyer should turn down a constitutional or criminal case simply because the client or cause is deemed politically incorrect, since—among other things—it will lead to the demise of civil liberties and the creation of a bar so divided along ideological lines that the defendants who most need legal representation will be relegated to ideologues who believe that politics and passion are a substitute for preparation and professionalism.

Several years ago, I got into a scrap with the Boston chapter of the National Lawyers Guild, a left-wing group that thought it was wrong to represent accused rapists. They changed their position only after an African American man was accused of serially raping white women, and the defendant claimed he was the victim of racist misidentification and profiling.

Free speech and criminal cases are different from cases that only involve continuing commercial gain from immoral conduct. A lawyer who provides ongoing legal assistance of a cocaine cartel is acting, in effect, as "consigliere" to a criminal conspiracy. A criminal organization has no legal right to ongoing advice on how to evade arrest and increase illegal profits. Many lawyers regard the cigarette industry as indistinguishable from the "mob" (though recent settlements suggest that even cigarette lawyers can sometime help their clients do the right thing, if only for self-serving reasons). Corporations that are not facing criminal charges do not have the same Sixth Amendment rights as accused criminals, nor should they have the same First Amendment rights as those confronting government censorship.[2] Still, we are all better off with a legal system under which important rights are not denied anyone without affording them the right to be defended by a zealous advocate. If we move away from the American tradition of lawyers defending those with whom they vehemently disagree—as we temporarily did during the McCarthy period and as we may be doing today—we weaken our commitment to the rule of law. What is popular today may be despised tomorrow. So beware of an approach that limits advocacy to that which is approved by the feeling of the day.

A recent case in Massachusetts places limits on a lawyer's discretion to decline a case. A feminist attorney who specialized in representing women in divorce cases refused to represent a male nurse's aide who was seeking financial support from his wealthy wife who was a doctor. The lawyer told the man that she did not accept male clients in divorce cases. A panel of the Massachusetts Commission against Discrimination ruled against the lawyer, stating "that an attorney [holding herself] out as open to the public may not reject a potential client solely on the basis of gender or some other protected class." Obviously, this situation is different from one in which a lawyer declines a case on political or ideological grounds, but it does suggest that lawyers are not entirely free to decline cases on any ground. In selecting clients, a lawyer may be a feminist but not a sexist. The distinction may be subtle, but it is real. Lawyers in Massachusetts, as in other states, are covered by civil rights and public accommodation laws, some of which prohibit discrimination based on religion creed, and political affiliation. Doctors and dentists are not free to turn away a patient who has AIDS or whose politics they despise. It is a fair question to ask why lawyers should have greater freedom to discriminate than do other professionals.

In the end, I hope lawyers will not need laws to tell them that they should represent those most in need of zealous advocacy, without regard to gender, race, ideology, economic situation, or popularity. Such an approach will make for a better legal system and a freer America.

---

2   But see Citizens United case.

The one thing a lawyer is never free to do is to accept a case and then pursue it without zeal. Although there are no specific criteria for measuring zeal, there certainly are general guidelines. Being someone's lawyer is different from being their friend. For a friend or relative, you may be willing to sacrifice your life, your liberty, or your fortune. You need not—and should not—do that for a client, even a client you like. Zealous advocacy has limits imposed by law, ethics, and common sense. We know what unzealous representation means: just look at some of the capital case lawyers in Alabama, Texas, and other Southern states! Several fell asleep during trial. (In one capital case I appealed, the lawyer fell asleep during the trial, but that was his finest hour, because when he was awake, he hurt his client by telling the jury that he didn't believe his own client's testimony!) Others conducted no investigation. (The same lawyer—a former Klansman representing a Black defendant accused of killing a white state trooper—refused to conduct any investigation in Black neighborhoods.) Many judges prefer unzealous to overzealous lawyers. That's why they appoint the former—who make their job easier, if they define their job as sentencing as many defendants as possible to death. Zealous lawyers—and lawyers deemed "overzealous" by some—are a pain in the ass to some judges. I know. I am one. We make their job harder by contesting every issue, demanding every right, and disputing every prosecutorial allegation, so long as it is in the best interest of the client (both short term and long term). That is the key to defining appropriately zealous advocacy: It must always be in the legitimate interest of the client. Its purpose is not to make you feel good or virtuous, but to help the client win by any ethical and lawful means.

I'm proud to be a criminal and constitutional defense lawyer who stands up to the government and defends people on principle, without regard to their possible guilt or innocence.

These are the principles I have always lived by. As Lillian Hellman, a former neighbor on Martha's Vineyard, said during the depths of McCarthyism: "I cannot and will not cut my conscience to fit this year's fashion." Today, far too many people fit their principles into partisan fashions.

CHAPTER 2

How Sticking to My Principles Got Me Cancelled

Three events occurred over the past several years that resulted in my cancellation by many individuals and institutions. They are as follows: (1) I defended President Trump against what I believe was an unconstitutional impeachment; (2) I defended Jeffrey Epstein and helped him get a favorable plea bargain; (3) I was falsely accused of having sex with a woman, connected to Epstein, who I never met. These are the <u>only</u> three events that would possibly explain the cancellations.[1] Some of the institutions have tried to concoct excuses—crowded calendars, changing priorities—but none has come up with any plausible justifications beyond the three new events for their refusal to host one of their most frequent past speakers. So let me describe these events and see if they in any way justify the cancellations.

As to the first two, I am proud of my role in carrying out my principles regarding due process, constitutional law, and the right to counsel. I did nothing wrong. I did nothing to be ashamed of. Those who cancelled me based on my principled representation of unpopular defendants have much to be ashamed of. I would do nothing different based on my principles.

---

1 I am referring to the events themselves, not the reporting—or misreporting—about them, which has given rise to lawsuits.

My defense of the Constitution on behalf of President Trump, was little different from what I did on behalf of Democratic officials and candidates for nearly half a century. I had previously helped defend President Bill Clinton against what I believe was an unconstitutional impeachment. I defended Democratic Senator Alan Cranston on the floor of the senate. I helped defend Senator Ted Kennedy at Chappaquiddick. I defended several Democratic congressmen, governors, mayors, attorneys general, district attorneys, political leaders and others. Some were accused of crimes ranging from murder, to bribery, to sexual misconduct and corruption. No one ever cancelled me or even condemned me for providing a zealous defense to those accused Democratic politicians.

My representation of Jeffrey Epstein was also not much different from my representation of other defendants who were accused of sexual misconduct. I won some, lost some, and arranged plea bargains for others. There was some criticism, but no cancellations or condemnations. Everyone seemed to acknowledge, sometimes grudgingly, that I was fulfilling my obligation as a defense lawyer under the Constitution, even if some were unhappy with the results.

But it was different with Trump and Epstein. Times were different. Attitudes had changed. Being perceived as "helping" or "enabling" clients who were viewed as "devils" and "beyond the pale," led many people to deploy the McCarthyite tactic of blaming the lawyer for the perceived sins of his client, and failing to see a difference between <u>supporting</u> the client's alleged <u>activities</u>, which I did not do, and <u>defending</u> the client's <u>rights</u>, which I proudly did.

It also led some people—primarily those who didn't know me—to believe, or want to believe, Virginia Giuffre's made-up accounts of having sex with me seven times in various and sundry places where I could not possibly have been during the relevant time periods. Some who hated me for representing Trump and Epstein <u>wanted</u> to believe, despite the evidence to the contrary, that I could have done what Giuffre falsely alleged. A small number even said that because of my defense of Trump and Epstein, I <u>deserved</u> to be accused of sexual misconduct, <u>even</u> if I was entirely innocent.

The demonstrable truth is that I never met Giuffre. I never in my life had sex with any underaged person. I have always conducted myself admirably when it comes to my sex life and my relationship with women. Over my 50-year career of teaching at Harvard Law School, not a single complaint has ever been leveled against me for inappropriate sexual behavior. Nor had any such complaint ever been leveled against me in any other context. My relationship with women has been exemplary. I did absolutely nothing wrong.

So, if I did nothing wrong in these matters, why was I cancelled? These are not gray area cases. There is no conceivable argument consistent with my principles and those shared by many other people, that I did anything blameworthy, certainly anything that would justify cancellation. In many cases of cancellation, the question is one of degree. The man admits he had sex with the woman, but claims it was consensual. The lawyer represented a client and there were allegations that he engaged in unethical behavior. None of those considerations are present in my situation. Again, I did nothing wrong.

The only reason why I have been cancelled for representing Trump and Epstein is that the cancellers disapproved of my clients. But lawyers have a special obligation to represent unpopular, even despised, clients. John Adams nearly ruined his political career by representing the British soldiers responsible for the Boston Massacre. Daniel Webster, Abraham Lincoln, Clarence Darrow, Thurgood Marshall, Edward Bennett Williams, and other distinguished lawyers represented clients who were even more despised than Trump and Epstein—if that is possible. And to answer an anticipated criticism: Yes, I am comparing myself (as others have compared me) to these great lawyers with regard to their decisions to represent "devils," "angels" and everyone in between. These lawyers, too, were condemned at the time but praised by the verdict of history, as I fully expect to be, when current passions cool. I also expect those who have cancelled me to be rightly condemned by the verdict of history. I may be overly optimistic, but I believe with Martin Luther King that "the arc of the moral universe is long, but it bends toward justice."

I challenge anyone to offer a substantive criticism of anything I did in either of those cases that warrants criticism or cancellation.[2] The fact that I helped produce outcomes favorable for my clients contributed to the hatred toward me, as had the favorable outcomes I helped achieve in the O. J. Simpson and Claus von Bülow cases. Many people told me that they had no objection to me defending these "scoundrels" but why did I have to win? My mother put it more directly when she was frequently confronted with the question: "Why does your son have to win cases for such bad people?" Her response: "The worse the person, the better the lawyer has to be to win the case." It is my responsibility as a lawyer to achieve the best lawful and ethical outcome, even if that outcome is not good for the rest of the world. As I wrote 40 years ago, quoting a source two centuries old:

> This is neither a radical nor a transient notion. As a British barrister named Henry Brougham put it in 1820:
> "An advocate, by the sacred duty which he owes his client, knows, in the discharge of that office but one person in the world, that client and none other. To save that client by all expedient means—to protect that client at all hazards and costs to all others, and among others to himself—is the highest and most unquestioned of his duties; and he must not regard the alarm, the suffering the torment the destruction which he may bring upon any other. Nay, separating even the duties of a patriot from those of an advocate, and casting them, if need be to the wind, he must go on reckless of the consequences, if his fate it should unhappily be, to involve his country in confusion for his client's protection."

---

2   CNN doctored the tape of me answering a question about whether a *quid pro quo* is impeachable. In my actual answer, I said it would be if it were "unlawful" or "illegal." CNN edited out that sentence and several of its commentators then lied and claimed that I had said a president could not be impeached even if his conduct was unlawful or illegal. Again, I did nothing wrong. I have sued CNN for defamation (see Chapter 11).

I have been attacked throughout my life for being a good defense lawyer who zealously defends his clients whether they were rich or poor, male or female, white or Black—guilty or not guilty. That is my job, and I will continue doing it as long as I have the strength to defend zealously.

So, I make no apologies for my choice of clients, for the tactics I employed and for the results I achieved. It is my critics and my cancellers who should be ashamed of themselves and who should be condemned, for violating the spirit of the Constitution and for discouraging young lawyers from taking on the thankless but important task of defending the most despised. Winston Churchill observed that nothing can be more abhorrent to democracy than to imprison a person or keep him in prison because he is unpopular. "This is the test of a civilization." He also said that "the mood and temper of the public in regard to the treatment of crime and criminals is one of the most unfailing tests of the civilization of any country." I am proud of my role as a defense attorney. I am proud of the fact that more than half of my cases have been done without any payment. I urge others to live by my principles when it comes to zealously defending the accused, whether rich or poor. I categorically reject any allegation that I did anything wrong, and I challenge my critics to show that I did.

In representing devilish characters, I have always lived by the implications of the following scene from the play and film *A Man for All Seasons*:

> **William Roper:** So, now you give the Devil the benefit of law!
> **Sir Thomas More:** Yes, What would you do? Cut a great road through the law to get after the Devil?
> **William Roper:** Yes, I'd cut down every law in England to do that!
> **Sir Thomas More:** Oh? And when the last law was down, and the Devil turned 'round to you, where would you hide, Roper, the laws all being flat? This country is planted thick with laws, from coast to coast, Man's laws, not God's! And if you cut them down, and you're just the man to do it, do you really think you could stand

upright in the winds that would blow then? Yes, I'd give the Devil
benefit of law, for my own safety's sake!

I will continue to "give the devil the benefit of law," <u>not</u> <u>only</u> for my
own sake but for that of our nation and our legal system.

As to the false accusation against me, what can I say? Again,
I did nothing wrong. I am the victim here—of a deliberately false
accusation. And victims should not be blamed or asked to apologize. I was never in the presence of my accuser. I never spoke to
her. I never touched her. I never flirted with her. And I certainly
never had any sexual contact with her. Nor did I engage in any
such conduct with anyone related to Jeffrey Epstein or any other
client. For those in doubt, let me briefly summarize the incontrovertible evidence that is thoroughly documented in my book *Guilt
by Accusation: The Challenge of Proving Innocence in the Age of the
#MeToo.*

When I was first falsely accused of having had sex with Virginia
Giuffre in Epstein's New Mexico ranch, his island, and other specified locations, I stated categorically that I have documentary records
that conclusively prove I could not have been in those locations
during the relevant time periods. I then produced cell phone records,
American Express charges, travel documents, recorded TV appearances, teaching schedules, calendars, court appearances, and other
documents. These documents were examined by Giuffre's own lawyers, who then stated that it was "not possible" for her account to
be true and that she was "wrong . . . simply wrong" in accusing me.
This statement is in a recorded conversation that has been validated
by law enforcement officials and acknowledged by the lawyer. We
then subpoenaed any emails that referred to me, but Giuffre denied
under oath that there were any. We then discovered that she did in
fact, have several "smoking gun" emails that proved she never met
me or even heard of me. The emails show that she had to be told by
a journalist friend—several years <u>after</u> she claimed to have had sex
with me on seven occasions—that I was a famous lawyer who had
represented Claus von Bülow and a "movie was made about that,"
and that my name "was a good name for your [book] pitch," even

though there was "no proof" I had done anything wrong. Giuffre then followed the journalist's advice and included my name in her book manuscript, <u>but</u> as a person she had once <u>seen</u>, but never <u>met</u> and certainly never had sex with.

She told her best friend, who she has known since childhood, that she did not want to accuse me but she "felt pressure" from her lawyers to do so. Her best friend also swore that Giuffre had never mentioned me during the time she was with Epstein, though she did mention other men. Giuffre told her best friend's husband that she never had sex with me. I have recordings of the friends confirming this.

Giuffre also told her best friend that she and her lawyers were going after the owner of Victoria's Secret for "at least half his money." He is Leslie Wexner, and he is worth close to 10 billion dollars. We then learned that at the same time Giuffre publicly accused me, her lawyers privately accused Wexner of nearly identical sexual misconduct and demanded a private meeting to resolve her "claims" against him. Both Wexner's wife and lawyer told me it was a "shakedown"—the word is recorded on tape. It seems obvious that I was being used as a stalking horse to send the unmistakable message to Wexner that if he didn't want to happen to him what happened to me—namely a very public accusation—there were private ways of resolving the matter, obviously implying the payments of hush money. This is certainly the way Wexner's wife and lawyer understood the message. After the lawyers for Giuffre and Wexner secretly met and presumably resolved the matter, Giuffre's lawyer appeared on TV and stated categorically that Wexner <u>did not</u> have sex with Giuffre—despite Giuffre's sworn testimony that she had sex with him on multiple occasions in multiple locations. In other words, two of Giuffre's lawyers have now confirmed—in recorded statements—that Giuffre was "wrong" in accusing Wexner and me. Legally that means she committed perjury, because she could not be honestly mistaken about having sex on multiple occasions with prominent individuals.

She also lied about how old she was when she met Epstein. At first, she said she was 14—well below the age of consent in any American state. She provided a vivid and detailed description of spending her "sweet sixteen" birthday with Epstein and Ghislaine Maxwell and receiving gifts from them. When employment records proved she was 17—above the age of consent in New York and other states—she admitted she had been "mistaken." She also admitted she was "mistaken" when she said she had dinner with Al and tipper Gore on Epstein's island. She had vividly described Gore and Epstein walking together on the island beach. The problem was that her lawyer, David Boies, had also represented Gore and knew she was lying about him. When it became clear that Gore didn't even know Epstein and had never been on his island, she was forced to retract that lie as well. Yet another lie, for which she was paid a large sum of money by a British tabloid.

The truth is that Giuffre is a serial liar who has accused many prominent men and women of sexual misconduct for money. She has obtained many millions of dollars from making these accusations. Among those she has accused are Senator George Mitchell, Ambassador Bill Richardson, Prime Minister Ehud Barak, Jacques Cousteau's granddaughter Alexandra, a president of a foreign country, and several other prominent billionaires. She has also said she was paid $15,000 by Epstein to have sex with Prince Andrew, when she was well above the age of consent, and that she was trained to be a prostitute! But her own lawyer has said on TV that based on his 11-year investigation, he does not believe that "any high-profile people" had sex with Giuffre. All of these high-profile people have categorically denied her accusations.

She has also admitted trafficking young women to Epstein, and one of her victims testified under oath that she was trafficked by Giuffre when she was 14. The government vouched for the credibility of Giuffre's victim by calling her as a witness in the Maxwell case but not calling Giuffre.

If her own lawyers don't believe her sworn accusation, how can others credit them? That is probably why the US Attorney's office that indicted Jeffrey Epstein and Ghislaine Maxwell deliberately omitted Giuffre as a witness. She had provided deposition testimony and media statements that were extremely incriminating of Epstein and Maxwell—if true. She would have been the key witness against both of them—if she were credible. But it is unethical for prosecutors to call a witness who they know, or believe, is not credible. So, they crafted the indictments carefully to charge misconduct primarily before Epstein and Maxwell ever met Giuffre, and after she left, but not concerning the period about which Giuffre could testify—if she were telling the truth.

So, in sum, there is no evidence corroborating Giuffre's accusations against me. On the day I was accused, I said there would be no pictures, even though she always carried a camera and photographed everything. I also said there could be no credible witnesses to something that did not occur. There is indisputable documentary evidence that it was not possible she was telling the truth about having sex with me in locations where I have never been to during the relevant time period. Her best friend and her best friend's husband know she is lying about me. Her own lawyers don't believe her. Prosecutors don't believe her. Yet, I have been cancelled based on her demonstrably false accusations.

Giuffre has now withdrawn the claim in her lawsuit that I ever had sex with her. She continues to sue me for defamation on the ground that I called her a "serial liar." (I am still suing her for having falsely said that I had sex with her.) She has admitted, however, telling numerous lies. She admitted making up numerous fake jobs on her resume, even relatively recently. She defended her repeated lies by saying she "had to do it"—fabricate events to get money—in order "to make it look as though I could be employed."

She falsely claimed to live in Florida and Colorado, in order to satisfy the "diversity" of citizenship requirement for a federal lawsuit, when she knew that she and her family actually lived in a large and expensive house in Australia. She "had to" give a phony Colorado address in order to obtain a Colorado driver's license and voting registration (thus committing the serious crime of voter fraud). She continued to claim she was 15 when she met and was trafficked by Epstein, despite seeing documentation that proved she was above the age of consent. She told many more lies, about the Gores, about not remembering the names of any of the children she repeatedly trafficked to Epstein, and about her "best friend" Rebecca.

We have also learned that in 2011, Giuffre tried to sell the memoir of her alleged sexual encounters to a publisher, who confirms that back then—several years after her claimed encounter with me—she said she didn't even know me! There are recordings that confirm this. Yet several years later—after her lawyers told her she could make money by accusing me—she "remembered" having had sex with me in numerous locations, where I never was during the relevant time. She "had to" lie about me, as she "had to" lie to get jobs, in order to make even more money.

Recently, Giuffre was deposed by my lawyers. She has demanded that her answers be sealed and kept from the public, as she has about other evidence of her mendacity. We are moving to have everything unsealed, so that everyone can judge for themselves whether to believe her, or whether she has indeed been a serial liar throughout her life and continues to lie because she "has to," in order to make even more money.

All in all, based on her own admissions and documentary evidence, she lied, sometimes under oath, on more than twenty occasions. If these multiple lies—all of which benefitted her—don't make her a "serial liar," both in fact and in law, it is difficult to know what would.

No reasonable person could actually believe, based on the evidence and lack thereof, that I ever had sex, or even met, Giuffre. Those who have cancelled me know that Giuffre is lying and that I am the totally innocent victim of her false accusations. They have told me so. But they did not want to be tainted even by false accusations, as I will demonstrate in the coming chapters.

The evidence conclusively proves that I am 100 percent innocent and without fault. There are no grey areas—no matter of degree. I could have done nothing different, other than refuse to represent Epstein and Trump, which would be inconsistent with my principles. Again, I challenge anyone, especially those who have cancelled me, to defend their McCarthyite conduct by pointing to one thing that

I did which I should not have done as a matter of principle.[3] They can't, and they won't.[4] Their silence condemns them, not me. So let me now turn to the cancellers.

3   I should never have agreed to be interviewed by Netflix which defrauded me into believing that they would show my evidence of Giuffre's history of lying. I provided the evidence and they refused to show it.

4   Larry David claims that he screamed at me because I put my "arm around Pompeo," and that I was part of the "whole enclave." As I explain in Chapter 4, Mike Pompeo was my former student and I approved of his role in the Middle East peace process.

CHAPTER 3

Being Cancelled by Jewish Institutions

Before I defended President Trump and Jeffrey Epstein, and before I was falsely accused by Virginia Giuffre, I was the second-most sought after speaker by Jewish organizations: synagogues, schools, book fairs, fundraisers pro-Israel rallies and the like. The most sought after was my dear friend and colleague Elie Wiesel.

For several years, I was the "defense lawyer" for Biblical characters who were put "on trial" at Temple Emanu-El in New York City, the most important Reform synagogue in the world. The trials—of Abraham, Moses, David, Noah, and others—were the most popular and well attended events at the Temple. In seeing the crowd, the rabbi commented, "This is like Yom Kippur." Upwards of 1,500 people would listen to the trial, and vote "guilty" or "not guilty." I was always the "defense attorney" and different "prosecutors" were selected to present the case against the "defendant." These prosecutors included Senator Joseph Lieberman, TV commentator Chris Cuomo, former Governor Eliot Spitzer, and others. King David was found guilty. All the others were found innocent. The audiences loved these trials, and the expectation was that they would continue for many years, culminating with "the Trial of God" Himself.

In the fall of 2019, the Trial of Joseph's brothers for selling Joseph to the Egyptians was scheduled and announced. A prosecutor was selected, and I was preparing my case. Then, the temple decided to be "cute" and make the trial "relevant' to current headlines. So they foolishly advertised it—without consulting with me—as the Trial of Joseph's brothers for "trafficking" Joseph. Several people objected to a trial of trafficking in light of the Epstein case. I suggested changing the advertising or coming up with a different Biblical character to put on trial—perhaps Job or Joshua. The temple decided, instead, to "postpone" the event. Rabbi Joshua Davidson assured me that the trials would resume the following year.

The following year was COVID and there were no in-person events at the temple. When public events resumed in the fall of 2021, I called the rabbi and asked him to schedule another trial. He said there would be no more trials. I asked why. He told me that the president and the board had decided against any more trials involving me. I then said I would be happy to speak on any other issue. I had recently written books on Israel, freedom of speech, and constitutional issues surrounding the vaccine mandates. He said he would get back to me. A few days later he informed me that the president and the board had decided that I could not speak at the Temple on any subject. He assured me that no one—certainly not he—believed that the sex charges were true, but they were in the media, and he implied that the Temple did not want to be identified with or tainted by any accusation, even if false.

I reminded the rabbi that this is exactly how McCarthyism worked in the 1950s. The institutions that banned people accused of being communists did not necessarily believe the accusations or think that they justified the ban, but they did not want to be tainted even by false accusations. So they went along with the ban—just to be safe.

The rabbi was obviously troubled by my cancellation. He told me that "rabbis don't make these decisions; the board and president do." He implied that if it were up to him, I would be invited. I responded that rabbis have an obligation not to accept unjust decisions by the lay president, and I offered to present my case to the board. He said that would not be possible. The board had made up its mind.

He then tried to justify the board's decision by concocting a transparently false rationale: The decision was made by the president of the board—a man named Harris Diamond—a retired ad executive for a company that advertised petroleum, surgary colas, alcoholic beverages, big pharma, and other questionable products. (The board also included Jeffrey Zucker who was forced out of CNN for an improper sexual relationship with an employee.) Diamond told the Rabbi he "didn't like my attitude toward the postponement of the Joseph trial!" It was a pretext and cover-up. I never spoke to Diamond or any member of the board. I agreed to what I was assured was merely a "postponement," and I made no criticism, public or private. The temple was simply not telling the ugly truth about why they cancelled me.

The result of the cancellation is that more than 1,500 people were denied the opportunity to see trials they loved and learned from. They were also denied the opportunity to hear my constitutional analysis of vaccine mandates. Most disturbingly, they were prevented from hearing—and having their children hear—my arguments in defense of Israel and against anti-Semitism at a time of increasing anti-Zionism and anti-Jewish attitudes in universities and among the hard left. I offered to speak on how to combat these dangers, but the temple preferred to hear from Peter Beinart, who advocates the end of Israel as the nation state of the Jewish people and who supports boycotts against Israelis. At the same time that I was cancelled, Beinart received a substantial speaking fee from the temple to make his case against Israel.

Temple Emanu-El has silenced my voice, while amplifying the voice of one of Israel's most toxic detractors. What does this say about the temple's priorities and values?

Moreover, the fact that I have been cancelled by a prominent Jewish institution gives cover to non-Jewish institutions—such as universities—to cancel me as well, without being accused of anti-Zionism or anti-Semitism. Temple Emanu-El has thus contributed to the silencing of my pro-Israel voice where it is most needed today. Shame on them.

Other synagogues will ask me to do the trials. I will agree, as long as the first title will be: "The Trial of Temple Emanu-El for Silencing an Influential Jewish Voice." This time, I will be the prosecutor, and I will invite Diamond or Rabbi Davidson to be the defense attorney—or to select a defender of their choice. If they decline, I will place an empty chair with the words "Temple Emanu-El—Defendant" where the defense attorney sits.

Silence is not the option in the face of unjustified McCarthyite censorship by a synagogue that claims to be a house of study, open-mindedness and Jewish values of dialogue and dissent. So I will continue to expose Temple Emanu-El's hypocrisy and cowardice.

Nor is Tempe Emanu-El the only prominent Jewish institution to cancel me. For more than a quarter of a century, I have been among the most sought after and popular speakers at the 92nd Street Y—the primary venue for Jewish talks in America. I have spoken there at least once a year and introduced nearly all of my new books there since I published *Chutzpah* more than 30 years earlier. I always fill the auditorium and get thousands of viewers on their feeds to synagogues and Jewish community centers around the world.

In 2019, I published *Defending Israel: The Story of My Most Challenging Client*. It was a natural fit for the 92nd Street Y. But when my agent approached them, they refused to allow me to speak. They, too, offered every phony excuse—crowded schedule, not enough interest. Finally, they admitted it: I had been banned because of the false accusation. They, too, said they didn't believe the accusation, but "we don't want trouble." Exactly what the practitioners of McCarthyism said when they complied with "blacklists," "red channels," and other bans on accused Communist and "fellow travelers."

This cancellation by the Y has been even more effective in silencing me than the cancellation by Temple Emanu-El, because talks at the Y are circulated more widely. So, their ban has prevented tens of thousands of people who would have wanted to hear my defense of Israel from doing so. And for what reason? Not because they believe I did anything wrong. They say they don't believe I did. But because they "don't want trouble." Shame, too, on the 92nd Street Y.

Other Jewish institutions have also followed Temple Emanu-El and the Y in banning me. This includes the Ramaz Jewish high school, which asked me to speak to the juniors and seniors to help prepare them for the anti-Zionism and anti-Semitism they can expect when they get to college. I agreed to speak. Then the headmaster called and told me that some people on the board did not want me to speak. So, the students were denied the opportunity to hear from the most experienced professor in dealing with university attitudes toward Israel—the person who has taught and spoken about Israel at more universities than anyone else.

When Amnesty International issued a 300-page blood libel against Israel, my response went unheard. For the first time, that bigoted organization claims that <u>all</u> of democratic Israel, not only the so-called occupied territories, is guilty of the international crime of apartheid. This attack is directed at Israel's right to exist as the nation state of the Jewish people. Previous attacks on Israel, such as those made by the Goldstone Report and former president Jimmy Carter, have been limited to specific actions or places. The Amnesty attack focuses on Israel's democracy and singles it out as an apartheid state comparable to white South Africa.

When the Goldstone and Carter attacks were leveled, I was asked to write detailed and credible responses. I did so and my rebuttals helped to destroy the credibility of these attacks. But now my voice has been silenced by major Jewish organizations.

The result is that mine is no longer as effective a voice against anti-Israel attacks such as those being leveled by Amnesty International. Before I was cancelled by Jewish organizations, I was regarded as "America's most public Jewish defender" and "Israel's single most visible defender—the Jewish state's lead attorney in the court of public opinion. These were not my assessments; these were the assessments of others. Unfortunately, no one else has replaced me.

I will continue to speak out for Israel. I will continue to defend Jewish victims of injustice around the world through organizations such as the Aleph Institute and others which have continued to support me. I will continue to stand against blood libels, but my voice will be muted. It will no longer be heard on college campuses around the world. Before this cancellation, I spoke on behalf of Israel on more college and university campuses than any other person. No more. I spoke to the media, wrote op-eds, published books, and devoted much of my time and energy to defending Israel. I can no longer do so as effectively as I once did. This is entirely the fault of major Jewish leadership, especially at the institutions that have cancelled me.

At 83 years old, I am still strong and able to defend myself. I will continue to do so. I ask for no pity for my situation. I can deal with false accusations against me, which I am doing by suing my false accusers. What I ask for is recognition that the leadership of the American Jewish community, has not only failed me, but has failed Israel and the Jewish community by becoming complicit in the McCarthyite cancellation of one of Israel's most effective voices.

In all of these cases, the McCarthyite censorship was blamed on nameless and faceless "board members" and "contributors." The rabbis, directors and principles always say they want me to speak, and they don't believe the accusations. But they don't control "the board," and "the board" doesn't want to hear from me. Those boards include many wealthy individuals with questionable pasts—financial, sexual, and moral. But money talks louder than principle. Tragically, that is how decisions—immoral, un-Jewish and indefensible—are made by many Jewish institutions that act without accountability, and against the interests not only of their members, but of the Jewish community in general.

So, the issue of my cancellation by prominent Jewish institutions after a lifetime of service to the Jewish community goes well beyond me as an individual. The disgraceful way in which I have been treated will deter young people from sacrificing for the Jewish community, from prioritizing the defense of Israel, from devoting time and energy to fighting anti-Semitism. Until I was unjustly cancelled, I served as a role model which young people were urged to emulate. I did nothing wrong. Yet the leadership of important Jewish institutions willingly threw me under the bus, silenced me, and distanced themselves from me without even giving me an opportunity to refute the false charges. What kind of message does this send to young Jews?

When Elie Wiesel heard of the false charges against me, he expressed outrage and hope that they would not silence my important voice. Had he lived long enough to see what these Jewish institutions have done, he would have been even more outraged as all decent people should be. I know that he would not have tolerated my unprincipled silencing. He would no longer have spoken at the venues that cancelled me, because he—unlike those who cancelled me—was a person of principle.

When prominent members of other minorities are falsely—or even truthfully—accused, the leaders of these groups generally come to their support, especially when the false accusers are not part of the group. At the very least, they give them a presumption of innocence and an opportunity to present their side of the story. Not so with the Jewish leaders who rushed to cancel me. Instead of supporting me against the lynch mob, they became part of the bullying mob, giving them cover and justification. Then they wonder why there are so few effective Jewish voices speaking on behalf of Israel and Jewish values. If they want the answer, they should look in the mirror. Or to quote Pogo: "We have seen the enemy and they are us!"

CHAPTER 4

Being Cancelled by Longtime Friends Because My Principles Did Not Fit Their Partisan Demands

N o one I know on Martha's Vineyard, where I have spent long summers for nearly half a century, believed the false sexual accusation against me. They know me and my family, and they have seen me interact with their families over many years. They know I don't flirt, touch, or do anything inappropriate with regard to sex. They see how close my wife and I are. And they know I would never do what Virginia Giuffre says I did with her. Her accusations played no part, as far as I can tell, in my cancellation by the group of old friends on Martha's Vineyard.

For most of them the issue was my constitutional defense of President Donald Trump—a man that many in this group regard as akin to Hitler. Literally! They constantly invoked that comparison. For some of them, and for millions of CNN viewers, it was CNN's decision to doctor the recording of my answer to the senators' question in order to make viewers falsely believe that I said that a president could commit crimes with impunity (see page 32).

The group on the Vineyard is comprised of several subgroups: A dozen or so people from Hollywood—actors, screenwriters, producers, director, agents; another dozen from the Boston area—doctors, lawyers, psychologists, business entrepreneurs, academics; a few mega-wealthy hedge fund operators, heirs, and some who married into wealth.

Prior to the Trump presidency, a small number would identify as radical leftists. Most were liberal Democrats, a few were moderate Republicans, and some were not particularly political. When Trump was elected, <u>every single one of them</u>—including me and my wife— were opposed to him and most of his policies, especially with regard to immigration, race, gender, and other hot button issues. Some didn't like Hillary Clinton, but none said—at least publicly—they would vote for Trump. I campaigned enthusiastically for Clinton, as I had for her husband.

Trump's election motivated many centrist liberals to "join the opposition"—i.e., to become radicalized, woke, and "progressive." The Trump presidency left little room for nuance calibration or selective support for some of Trump's policies or actions. You were either part of "the opposition" or part of "the enablers." You were a "true Scotsman" or an enemy of "true Scotsman."

I could never be a "true Scotsman" on any issue or for any ide- ology. I always try to think through issue and decide for myself on the right position. This is true of Israel, liberalism, constitutional rights, and every other political and social issue about which I care deeply. The only matters about which I am a true Scotsman relate to my wife, children, grandchildren, and closest friends. To them I am <u>loyal</u>, and my loyalty transcends my political and ideologi- cal principles. For everything else, my principles come first. As to them, loyalty <u>is</u> my principle. I am <u>not</u> loyal to a particular party, country, philosophy, religion, or anything else. As to those, I judge each on their merits and demerits. I do <u>not</u> judge my family and closet friends. I love them and am loyal to them regardless of the merits of what they do or believe. I may disagree with them. I may argue with them. I will try to get them to change their minds, when I think they are wrong. But I don't judge them or dilute my loyalty to them.

To the group on the Vineyard, loyalty and principle required choosing sides, regardless of the merits of any particular argument or position. Agreeing with <u>anything</u> Trump did, said, or wanted was blasphemy. I am reminded of the fundamentalist Christian concept of being "a fool for Christ"—of suspending rationality to demonstrate total submission to God's will. In relation to Trump, total opposition was required, regardless of the law, the Constitution or the merits of a particular position. One had to be "a fool" against everything Trump stood for, even if he was occasionally correct.

Early in the Trump administration, I realized I could not go along with the Vineyard mindset. It began when President Trump asked for my help on efforts to resolve the enduring conflict between Israel and the Palestinians. Previous presidents, both Democrats and Republicans, had asked for my assistance because I am close to many Israeli leaders. I have always agreed, and I agreed to help President Trump and his team. It was the right thing to do.

I strongly supported his recognition of Jerusalem as Israel's capital, and his recognition of Israel's annexation of the Golan Heights. Indeed, I suggested arguments in support of these recognitions, some of which Trump quoted. I advised on the Trump Peace Plan and the Abraham Accords. I also supported his executive decree against anti-Semitism on university campuses, and spoke in favor of it—calling it a game changer—at the White House. I opposed closing the US Consulate in East Jerusalem, which served Palestinian residents. I was not a true Scotsman even on Trump's policies toward Israel.

I also opposed Trump's so-called (and misnamed) "Muslim ban," which limited entry into the United States from certain majority Muslim countries (but not others). I predicted correctly how the Supreme Court would rule on its constitutionality.

When the Democrats decided to impeach Trump on the grounds of "abuse of power" and "obstruction of Congress," I argued that neither of these grounds were specified in the Constitution ("Treason, bribery, or other high crimes and misdemeanors"), and were thus unconstitutional. I pointed out that most of our presidents—including Washington, Jefferson, Lincoln, Roosevelt, Reagan, and Obama—had been accused by members of Congress of "abuse of power," which is an open-ended and subjective concept capable of partisan abuse. Hamilton and Madison had specifically objected to any formulation that would invite such abuse. I wrote articles and argued in the media against the constitutionality of impeaching the president against whom I had voted and against whom I intended to vote in 2020.

But that was not enough for the Vineyard crowd. I refused to be their "good Scotsman." Instead, by opposing Trump's impeachment on solid constitutional grounds, I became his "enabler," and thus a "traitor" to "the opposition."

Instead of discussing our differences or trying to convince me I was wrong, they simply cut me off. Some of them simply lacked the capacity to understand how a liberal constitutional lawyer could oppose Trump and his politics, and yet defend his constitutional rights. Others were capable of understanding, but chose not to. I don't know which is worse.

On one occasion a Hollywood producer, whose daughter I had helped avoid college discipline, and who had, in turn, encouraged our actress daughter, was on the porch of the Chilmark store, where we frequently congregated for lunch. I said hello. He turned his back and walked away.

On another occasion, one of the group—a moderate Republican—was seen having coffee with me. He told me he received six calls from other members of the group, asking why he was willing to speak to me and implying that he would not be welcome if he continued.

The wife of a hedge fund guy—whose daughter I helped not to be suspended from high school—dramatically walked out of a dinner party when she saw my wife and me at the table. A prominent political figure was somewhat more polite. She did not walk out but said "I wouldn't have agreed to come if I had known you were invited."

A lawyer who had repeatedly begged me to refer cases to him, wrote me the following email when I presented the president's constitutional case to the Senate: "Your contribution to and validation of our president, the pusillanimous Republican senators, and a trial that was no more than a sham, is so repugnant to me, that it is better we no longer share each other's society." This, after a quarter of a century of sharing each other's society (whatever that means). Others followed suit. The crowd had formed. Groupthink, or lack of think, took over. Anyone who didn't go along was not a good Scotsman.

I was cancelled not only by individuals, but by the Chilmark Library, the book fair, the community center, and the Hebrew center. I had spoken every year to overflow crowds at the library, but the librarian told me the crowds were "too large for our small library to handle." This was perhaps the most dishonest of the many dishonest excuses given by these centers of learning and thought for cancelling one of their most popular speakers.

My cancellation received widespread media coverage, none of which I generated. My encounter with Larry David on the porch of the Chilmark store in the summer of 2021 is a perfect example. First a few words about my long-standing association with Larry. I met him in the 1990s on the Vineyard and we became summer friends, with an occasional get-together in Los Angeles and New York City. He came often to our Vineyard home for dinner. He exercised in our basement gym. We shared laughs on the Chilmark porch over pizza and we played volleyball together. When he began *Curb Your Enthusiasm* in 1999, he used me as his unofficial consultant on all things Jewish and legal. He asked me whether Orthodox Jews really have sex through a hole in the sheet. I said no. He asked me about circumcision, about being alone with a woman who is not one's wife, and other such issues.

One day I was in the British House of Lords about to make a speech when he called me on my cell phone. I told him I couldn't talk, but he insisted it was a "show emergency." I asked him what the emergency was, and he said he membered that I once had a case in which a woman had called one of her employees a "d..k," and he had responded by calling her a "c..t." "I need to know how the case came out. Is the c-word worse than the d-word, or are they equivalent?" I reminded him that I was in the hallowed hall of the House of Lords and couldn't say those words. He insisted, and so I told him the c-word was worse. He was grateful.

Larry liked my books and wrote blurbs for several of them, such as this:

Dershowitz has done it! A non-fiction book (not about baseball) that I actually read—and understood. The man must sleep in sub-freezing temperature to keep his brain that fresh. If he had been my professor, I might have become a philosopher—or, God forbid, a lawyer. Now I will set about the business of taking this newfound knowledge and trying to pass it off as my own.

He spoke at the dinner honoring me for my work on human rights, and Larry and his wife asked me to represent them, pro bono, in several disputes and I did. I also tried to mediate a controversy they were involved in with another person in our group. When a relative was having trouble getting into college, he begged me to try to help her. I did, and she was admitted to the college of her choice.

That was the nature of our relationship—not a close friendship but a long-term acquaintanceship that we both enjoyed—until Trump became president. Then everything changed. At the beginning, he spoke to me occasionally, always about why I was wrong to be in any way associated with Trump, and how it was affecting our friendship. But after I presented the constitutional case against Trump's first impeachment, he became furious at me.

One day during the summer of 2021, when Trump was already out of office, I was having a cup of coffee with a left-wing lawyer friend, who is not part of the Chilmark "group." Although he despises Trump and favored his impeachment, he did not end his friendship with me. (Nor did other hard left older radicals, some of whom experienced, or at least remember, the scourge of McCarthyism.) I was wearing my favorite Chilmark T-shirt, which my wife had ordered for me. It read: "It's the Constitution Stupid." I wore another T-shirt over it to show my lawyer friend, who constantly complained to me that he had been rejected by Harvard Law School. It read: "Harvard Law (just kidding)." I planned to give it to him as a gift to celebrate his son's recent admission to Harvard Law School. He declined the gift, so I was wearing both shirts, when Larry pulled up to the Chilmark store. He walked past me as he left the store, after buying a few items, and I said hello. He turned away. I then said: "We can still talk, Larry." To which he replied: "No, no. we really can't. I saw you with your arm around [former Trump Secretary of State Mike] Pompeo. It's disgusting." I tried to explain that Pompeo was my former student, and I was showing support for his efforts to make peace in the Middle East. But he cut me off: "It's disgusting. Your whole enclave—it's disgusting. You're disgusting."

I then took off my Harvard T-shirt to show him my Constitution T-shirt, but he stormed away, still screaming about how "disgusting" I was.

Unbeknownst to either of us—who were not expecting to encounter each other—someone who was on the porch wrote down the words of the confrontation and sent them to Page 6 of the *New York Post*, which reported them. What they failed to report was the genuine, deep, and emotional anger manifested by Larry. His face turned red, his veins bulged, and I worried that he might have a stroke. It was as if he had encountered Trump himself. It made me understand how strongly and viscerally some anti-Trump zealots feel. But I'm sure that many McCarthyites felt as strongly about communists in the 1950s. That is not an excuse for associating lawyers with their clients, whether Trump or communists.

Larry David himself is not important, but he is typical of the thoughtless, knee-jerk attitude of many who were once tolerant liberals, and who have now become intolerant McCarthyites in reaction to the Trump presidency. Among the first casualties of extremism is principle. Former friends who have cancelled me justify it by accusing me of picking the wrong side. None has ever accused me of violating any principle. To the contrary, they have accused me of putting my principles ahead of the need to be rid of Trump. They are correct in that regard.

CHAPTER 5

Now Trump Supporters Have Turned on Me for Opposing Biden's Impeachment

I began writing the book that became *The Case Against Impeaching Trump* in the summer of 2016—before the election. At that time, it looked like Hillary Clinton would be elected. Some influential Republicans were already preparing to impeach her vowing that they would begin impeachment proceedings "the day she is sworn in." They pointed to statements made by James Comey, the director of the FBI, criticizing her use of private emails, her role in the Benghazi disaster, and other allegedly impeachable offenses committed before she was inaugurated. I began to draft a constitutional defense on the ground that <u>none</u> of these accusations even if true, rose to the level of an impeachable "high crimes and misdemeanors." The title of my proposed book was *The Case Against Impeaching Hillary Clinton*. My publisher even created a mock cover with that title.

I strongly believe that the Republicans would have tried to impeach Hillary Clinton—as they had impeached her husband—had she won.

Well, Trump won. The shoe was now on the other foot. And true to the partisan hypocrisy that dominates politics, some Democratic leaders sought to impeach Trump, deploying the very argument they would have opposed had Hillary Clinton been elected and impeached, an argument similar to those they made against the impeachment of Bill Clinton. Professor Laurence Tribe demanded Trump's impeachment even <u>before</u> he was sworn in! Likewise, some Republicans deployed arguments in defense of Trump that they would have rejected if Hillary Clinton were being impeached, and that they had rejected when Bill Clinton was impeached.

We know what happened—to Trump, to the media, to politicians, and to me! So now Joseph Biden is president. Yes, he won fair and square.

Now some Republicans are advocating Biden's impeachment for his decisions regarding the timing of the removal of American troops from Afghanistan, his policies on the Mexican border, his vaccine mandate, his policies with regard to Ukraine, and other controversial issues. Though his actions, whatever one may think of them, do not meet the constitutional criteria for impeachment, some of the same Republicans who strongly opposed President Trump's unconstitutional impeachment now support Biden's conviction and removal.

Both are wrong as a matter of constitutional law. But because I now oppose Biden's impeachment, I am getting hate messages from Trump supporters that mirror the ones I got from Trump haters when I opposed his impeachment. They call me a "partisan hack," a "turncoat," a cowardly Democrat, and a "Democratic apologist." It's a fascinating window into a thoughtlessly, pathologically divided America.

The anti-Biden emails and calls began just like the anti-Trump ones did: "I used to admire you but now I'm so disappointed in you." Or "You were once my hero but now you're a villain." Some are much less polite.

My responses are also the same: "You never should have admired me because I was never on your side politically. I'm a non-partisan defender of the Constitution, and people like you only admire partisans who they think are on their side. So, you wrongly admired me when you thought I was defending Trump's constitutional rights because I supported Trump politically, but you are disappointed in me now because you wrongly think I'm supporting Biden's constitutional rights because I support him politically."

Both sets of admirers-detractors are mistaken. In fact, I opposed most (but not all) of Trump's policies. And I support most (but not all) of Biden's policies. But that has absolutely nothing to do with my views about whether they committed impeachable offenses. Unlike some purportedly objective constitutional "scholars"—such as Professor Tribe—I base my views of impeachment on neutral views of the text and history of that document, not on whether a particular interpretation will help or hurt my party or pollical ideology. I always apply the "shoe on the other foot" test: Would my interpretation be the same if applied to the other side of the partisan divide?

That's why, as a liberal Democrat who voted for Hillary Clinton, I opposed President Trump's impeachment. It was based on accusations—"abuse of power" and "obstruction of Congress"—that did not satisfy the constitutional criteria of "treason, bribery or other high crimes and misdemeanors." Had Hillary Clinton been elected and impeached on those grounds, I would have defended her as well. Indeed, I predicted back then that the unconstitutional partisan weaponization of impeachment by the Democrats would be turned against the next Democratic president. And now it has—by hypocritical Republicans who opposed impeaching Trump on similarly unconstitutional grounds.

I'm not surprised, because partisanship generally trumps principle in Washington—as it did when Republicans killed President Obama's nomination of Merrick Garland to the Supreme Court ostensibly because it was an election year, and then confirmed Trump's nominee much closer to the election.

We are quickly becoming a tribal nation where everyone is expected to support everything their tribe supports and oppose everything it opposes, regardless of the merits or the Constitution. Principled decision-making regardless of party has become an anachronism for many politicians. Their excuse is: "They did it first." That may well be true of many issues, but it is no excuse for either side. Two constitutional wrongs do not make a right. To the contrary, they are twice as bad as one.

Biden will not be impeached on the current record, but that is only because the Republicans do not currently have the votes. If they were to take over the House in 2023, he might well be impeached, regardless of the constitutional merits or demerits. This is precisely the "greatest danger" that Alexander Hamilton worried about: that "the decision [regarding impeachment] will be regulated more by the comparative strength of parties, than by the real demonstrations of innocence or guilt."

Both parties must stop weaponizing the impeachment power for partisan purposes. The framers sought to limit this power to criminal-type behavior akin to treason and bribery, not to policy differences or even "maladministration" of office, which was explicitly rejected as a ground for impeachment.

President Trump was not removed from office through the constitutional mechanism of impeachment. He was removed by the voters. Republicans who want to see President Biden removed should try to persuade voters, not distort the Constitution, as Democratic members of Congress did with regard to President Trump. And the media should call these issues straight, without the thumb of partisanship and ideology on its reportorial scale.

We, the American public, are entitled to principled decision-making by all branches of government, by the media, by academics, by each other. Instead, we are getting partisan hypocrisy.

CHAPTER 6

How Identity Politics is Replacing Principle in Our Courts of Law

The statute of justice blindfolded reflects the biblical admonition to judges not to recognize faces. Justice must be blind to identity. This is especially true in criminal cases, which should be decided <u>solely</u> on the basis of the evidence and the law. The <u>only</u> question is whether the state has proved <u>this</u> defendant's guilt, under existing law, beyond a reasonable doubt. His or her race, ethnicity, gender, sexual orientation, political affiliation, celebrity, or name should not matter. Nor should those of his alleged victim. But too often, they not only matter, they determine the outcome of the case. How many times have we heard: "If his name were John Smith, rather than [fill in the blank], he would have been acquitted."

Even if a broader social good would be achieved by an unlawful verdict, such a verdict should never be permitted. There is no place for civil disobedience or affirmative action to achieve a higher good in the criminal justice system. Even if the lawfully required verdict is <u>unjust</u>, it must be rendered, if it is the <u>correct</u> one <u>legally</u>. A famous—some may say infamous—exchange between Judge Oliver Wendell Holmes and his law clerk illustrates this counterintuitive imperative under the rule of law:

Law Clerk: But your honor, this decision does not do justice.

Holmes: Young man, we are not in the justice business. We are in the law business.

The legislature can change the law prospectively, not retroactively, to secure better justice in the future. But a criminal defendant must be tried under the then <u>existing</u> law, for his conviction to be constitutionally valid. Under the rule of law, justice can be achieved only if the law is followed, especially in criminal cases.

Today, criminal trials are seen as "sending messages," "achieving reparations for past injustices"—even as "affirmative action." A case I played a role in contributed to this distortion of the rule of law.

In the O. J. Simpson case, Johnnie Cochran asked the jury: "to send a message." I disapproved and said so. Many people picked sides in that case based more on race than evidence. Some said that so many white murderers had been set free, that it was time for a possibly guilty Black man to be set free as well. People applauded or denounced the verdict based on race. Cochran was accused by a member of the defense team of "playing the race card," and "dealing it from the bottom of the deck." That may have been too harsh, because defense counsel must play every ethically possible card. But there is little doubt that race played a role in the case, just as it had in the earlier Rodney King and subsequent police shooting cases.

Identity politics in general and race in particular, have played significant roles in recent high-profile cases, such as those involving George Zimmerman, Derek Chauvin, Kim Potter, Kyle Rittenhouse, and Travis McMichael. Although the facts and law in the cases varied considerably, there was a common theme: racial justice is more important—to ideologues, the media, and politicians—than the individual merits of a given case.

I wrote and spoke about these cases as they were occurring or shortly thereafter. What follows is based largely on what I wrote in real time, with current comments added.

A. George Zimmerman

Shortly after George Zimmerman shot Trayvon Martin in what a Florida jury later concluded was a legitimate act of self-defense,

President Obama sent a very public message to Martin's parents—"if I had a son he would look like Trayvon." The evidence that was subsequently revealed suggests, however, that if the Obamas had a son, he certainly wouldn't have acted like Trayvon Martin did in the moments before he was killed.

Martin was killed by a bullet fired by Zimmerman. The issue in the court of public opinion was who was at fault for the death of the 17-year-old Black youth. The issue in the criminal case was whether the prosecution could prove beyond a reasonable doubt that Zimmerman did not fire the single shot in self-defense—that is, because he reasonably feared for his physical safety.

These two very different issues were constantly confused by the media, the talking heads, and even some lawyers who should have known better.

Most striking was the apparent error—though it is hard to believe it was inadvertent—made by NBC's local affiliates and then *The Today Show*. NBC edited a video clip to have George Zimmerman say the following during his call to the police: "This guy looks like he's up to no good. He looks Black." There was no indication that anything came between the first sentence and the second sentence. Indeed, the very thrust of the quote, as edited and played on the air, is that Zimmerman concluded that Martin was no good because "he looks Black." Here is what the actual unedited tape says:

> **GZ:** [George Zimmerman] This guy looks like he's up to no good. Or he's on drugs or something. It's raining and he's just looking around.
> **SPD:** Okay and this guy, is he Black, white or Hispanic?
> **GZ:** He looks Black.

Thus, Zimmerman's reference to Martin being Black came only after he was asked a direct question about the race of the suspect by the police operator. He then responded to the question, as any person—Black or White, egalitarian or racist—would do under the circumstances.

The perception that Zimmerman made a racist comment pervaded the media for a considerable period of time before NBC finally acknowledged its grievous and apparently intentional "mistake." What NBC did to Zimmerman was remarkably similar to what CNN did to me, when they doctored a recording of what I said during my opposition to President Trump's impeachment. I first emphasized that a president <u>could</u> be impeached if he engaged in quid pro quo that "were in some way <u>illegal</u>" or "<u>unlawful</u>." CNN deliberately edited—doctored—the recording to omit the words "illegal" and "unlawful," and then had their commentators say it was my opinion that a president could not be impeached <u>even</u> if he did something <u>illegal</u> or <u>unlawful</u>. Precisely the <u>opposite</u> of what I actually said. CNN has not apologized.

There were other similar mistakes in the Zimmerman case as well. The prosecutor deliberately submitted what I believed was, in effect, a perjured affidavit in an effort to get the judge to approve a murder charge. The affidavit willfully omitted any reference to the potentially life-threatening injuries sustained by Zimmerman allegedly at the hands of Martin in the moments before the shooting.

Before she submitted the probable cause affidavit, Prosecutor Angela Corey was fully aware that Zimmerman had sustained serious injuries to the front and back of his head at the hands of Martin, who apparently beat his head against the hard ground. The affidavit said that her investigators, "reviewed reports, statements, and photographs that purportedly detail[ed] the following." It went on to describe "the struggle," but it deliberately omitted all references to Zimmerman's injuries, which were clearly visible in the photographs she and her investigators reviewed.

The judge, in deciding whether there is probable cause to charge the defendant with second-degree murder, should not have been kept in the dark about physical evidence that is so critical to determining whether a homicide occurred, and if so, a homicide of what degree. By omitting this crucial evidence, Corey deliberately misled the court.

Corey seemed to believe that our criminal justice system is like a poker game in which the prosecution is entitled to show its cards only after the judge has decided to charge the defendant with second-degree murder.

That's not the way the system is supposed to work and that's not the way prosecutors are supposed to act. That a prosecutor would hide behind the claim that she did not have an obligation to tell the whole truth until after the judge ruled on probable cause displays a kind of gamesmanship in which prosecutor should not engage.

Nor was this Prosecutor Corey's last dirty trick. By the close of the evidence at trial, it was clear to nearly everyone—except some legal talking heads on television—that the prosecution had not satisfied its burden of proof. It couldn't because in the absence of video or eyewitness evidence, no one knew for sure who threw the first punch, who was yelling for help, and who was endangering who. The absence of such evidence demonstrates reasonable doubt. So the prosecutors tried, a the last minute, to move the goalposts. They asked the judge to instruct the jurors that they could convict Zimmerman of third-degree murder if they concluded that he had engaged in "child abuse"—an absurd claim not supported by any evidence. This might allow the jurors to reach a compromise verdict and save face for the prosecutors. The judge correctly rejected this desperate, and in my view unethical, ploy. The jury then unanimously acquitted Zimmerman.

The defense tried to demonize Trayvon Martin by raising the young man's mixed school record, minor criminal history, and other characteristics not unusual for teenagers. These characteristics, because they were largely unknown to Zimmerman when he fired his gun, were of questionable relevance at the trial, except to the extent that they show a young man trained in martial arts and capable of causing considerably bodily harm to Zimmerman.

The Zimmerman-Martin case was among the most racially divisive tragedies in recent history. Who was more at fault can never be known with absolute certainty because of lack of witnesses, videos, or other evidence of crucial events surrounding the shooting. But it can be known with relative certainty whether under the evidence presented in court, the jury rendered the correct legal verdict. It did.

B. The Derek Chauvin Case

In the Chauvin case, there were both witnesses and videotapes.

The video of former Minneapolis police officer Derek Chauvin keeping his knee on the neck of the dying George Floyd for more than nine minutes is among the most powerful pieces of evidence I have ever seen. It indisputably shows Chauvin keeping his knee on Floyd's neck as Floyd submissively lies handcuffed, telling Chauvin he can't breathe and calling for his mother. Numerous witnesses at the scene kept demanding that Chauvin get his knee off Floyd's neck as Floyd clearly slips into unconsciousness.

Floyd did not resist or fight back. He simply struggled to breathe— until he died.

Some bystanders tried to get closer to Floyd, but other police officers stood in the way and stopped them. The evidence of Chauvin's <u>moral</u> culpability is overwhelming and beyond dispute. He deserves no pity or compassion.

But he does deserve justice.

Chauvin's <u>legal</u> guilt poses an entirely different series of questions: Did he intend to kill Floyd? Did he realize that death could have resulted from keeping his knee on Floyd's neck? Was he reckless in not removing his knee? Would Floyd have died from Chauvin's knee if not for the drugs in his system or a heart condition?

These and other questions were decided by jurors, after hearing all of the evidence and arguments and being instructed by the trial judge. The guilty verdict is being appealed. But the moral, political, and ideological issues seem black and white: No police officer should <u>ever</u> do what Chauvin did to a man who was subdued, was lying on the ground, was unarmed, and was surrounded by five armed officers. The tape alone, without more, compels that conclusion.

If the Minneapolis police guidelines allow such conduct, they must be changed. The video speaks louder than any effort to justify Chauvin's actions.

Now let us imagine how different the situation would be if there had been no cellphone videos—if it had been the word of the police officers against those of the largely Black bystanders. Many such cases have occurred over the past several years. Some have been taped, others not. The recording in this case, and in others, has made all the difference.

As a civil libertarian, I realize that the pervasiveness of cellphone cameras is sometimes a double-edged sword. On the positive side, it documents police abuses and other evils that would otherwise be difficult to prove. On the negative side, the pervasiveness of these cameras threatens all of our privacy, if used promiscuously and without consent or knowledge.

In one sense, it's meaningless to debate the pros and cons of any new technology, because no matter what we say, the reality is that tech will advance, improve, and become increasingly interwoven with our lives. The law can do something, but not much, to control its misuse. We must acknowledge that with every technological innovation, we lose a little bit of privacy, autonomy, and dignity. (Just ask Jeffrey Toobin.)

The bottom line is, we must learn to live with the new technology. The law will always be playing catch-up but will never succeed in actually catching up with advancing technology.

The Chauvin case demonstrates the positive use of cellphone video cameras. The video of Chauvin refusing to lift his knee off the neck of the dying Floyd has changed the world. It will never be the same. And it should never be the same. What we see on that video is a vision of hell that cannot be allowed to become or remain the new normal, the old normal, or any version of normal.

So two cheers for video cameras.

Following the guilty verdict in the Chauvin case, I said that there was sufficient evidence to convict of homicide, but wondered if the appellate courts might reverse the conviction based on juror intimidation by Congresswoman Maxine Waters and others. So stay tuned.

C. Kim Potter

Police Officer Kim Potter was charged with manslaughter in the tragic death of Duante Wright, whom she shot with a gun she mistakenly fired believing it was a Taser. The Minnesota statute provides that "A person who causes the death of another by any of the following means is guilty of manslaughter in the second degree . . .

(1) by the person's culpable negligence whereby the person creates an unreasonable risk, and consciously takes chances of causing death or great bodily harm to another." The crucial evidence in this case is the videotape of the encounter, which clearly shows that Potter intended to tase Wright, rather than shoot him. As she draws her weapon, she can be heard screaming "Taser, Taser, Taser." She then fires once from what she clearly believed was a non-lethal Taser. She quickly realizes that she has mistakenly fired a lethal pistol and shouts, "Holy s**t, I just shot him."

There is simply no way that a reasonable and properly instructed jury could conclude beyond a reasonable doubt that Potter "consciously" took the chance of causing Wright's death. She did not intend to kill him, nor did she consciously believe her decision to tase him would produce a lethal result. Nor could it find that she violated first-degree manslaughter statues, which also requires a state of mind that the prosecution did not prove.

How then could a reasonable prosecutor charge a police officer— one with 26 years of experience and a good record—with violating statutes that simply don't cover her conduct? No conscientious prosecutor could do so, but the crowds demanding justice for Daunte Wright put a heavy thumb—indeed an elbow—on the scales. This was a charge based not on the rule of law, but on the demands of the crowd and the race of the victim.

There are three theories that the prosecution could have presented in an effort to justify their unjust decision to charge Potter. None of them work as a matter of fact or law.

The first follows the text of the statute but stretches the facts to fit it. Prosecutors might try to argue that Potter knew full well she was firing a lethal weapon rather than a Taser and shouted "Taser" as a cover for consciously taking action that she knew might cause Wright's death. But there is absolutely no evidentiary support for such a speculative theory, and the prosecution did not put it forward, though some extremists did.

The second theory the prosecution could have offered is that although Potter intended to use the taser, even that action violated the statute, because tasers carry a small chance of causing death or great bodily harm. But to make that argument, prosecutors would have had to show that firing a taser under the circumstances of this encounter was criminal. We know Potter was aware that Wright was wanted on an outstanding felony warrant. We don't know (or at least I don't know) how much she knew about the underlying felony. We now know that it was attempted armed robbery involving the use of a gun. We are also advised that Wright continued to possess a gun after he was arrested for armed robbery. But even if Potter was not aware of these facts at the time she decided to use the Taser, her decision would seem entirely justified: a wanted felon was trying to get into his car, which could have contained a weapon. He was also trying to drive away, thus potentially endangering another officer and pedestrians and evading his capture. Under these circumstances the use of the Taser would seem justified. It certainly would not be criminal under the terms of the homicide statute.

Third, prosecutors might try to interpret the statute in a way that substitutes "or" for "and." As written, the statute requires that the defendant's "culpable" negligence presents an "unreasonable" risk "*and*" consciously takes chances of causing death or serious bodily harm. If one changes "and" to "or," the prosecution could argue that Potter engaged in culpable negligence which created an unreasonable risk—without having to prove that she was consciously aware she might cause death or bodily harm. But it is unconstitutional to change a statute after the events in question so as to make its words fit the facts of a case. A criminal statute must be clear and unambiguous as interpreted by the usual rule of statutory interpretation and grammar. Thomas Jefferson once put this requirement as follows: A criminal statute must be so clear that the ordinary person will be able to understand it when reading it while running. I taught criminal law for half a century and studied hundreds of criminal statutes, and I cannot understand this statute as eliminating the requirement of conscious knowledge that there was a chance of causing death or bodily harm.

If I were teaching this case in my criminal law class, I would ask the students about several hypotheticals:

1. What if Potter had fired her Taser and stopped Wright with no permanent damages? Would this be a crime?
2. If not, what if the Taser accidentally killed Wright? Would that be a crime?
3. What if Potter intended to shoot and kill Wright with her revolver, but inadvertently reached for her Taser and merely tased him? Would she be guilty of attempted murder?

The answer to the first two hypos is almost certainly no, because tasing a dangerous fleeing felon is not criminal, even if he dies as a result of an unknown medical condition. The answer to the third hypo is probably yes, because criminal culpability for attempted crimes generally turns on the intent of the shooter, rather than the result. The same should be true of the first two hypos.

Notwithstanding the law and the facts, the jury convicted Potter of manslaughter and the judge denied her bail pending appeal—a double injustice.

Officer Potter, a decorated policewoman with more than two decades of service, simply did not commit a crime. The prosecution conceded that she did not intend to shoot Wright and that she made a mistake by pulling out and firing a gun instead of a Taser.

Under American law, honest mistakes are not crimes—even if they result in tragic deaths. For example, a driver accidently putting a foot on the gas instead of the brake and killing a child is not necessarily a crime. It becomes a crime only if the action was reckless, involving a conscious decision to engage in conduct which the defendant knows poses a high risk of serious injury or death.

Every American, regardless of race or political persuasion, should be concerned when a decent police officer is indecently charged and convicted for making the kind of honest mistake that any person could make when confronted with the pressures of an immediate life-or-death decision. Police officers will be disincentivized by this decision to take actions which may be necessary to protect innocent life.

Only rarely do police officers actually fire their guns or their Tasers, but sometimes such action is necessary. When action is taken under circumstances such as those faced by Officer Potter, occasional honest mistakes are inevitable—and such mistakes could go both ways. What if Potter had failed to stop Wright and he had gotten back behind the wheel and killed another officer as well as several pedestrians? That, too, would have been an honest mistake.

Criminal law is supposed to apply to bad people consciously making bad decisions, that they know or should know are in violation of the law. It should not apply to good police officers who make honest decisions that turn out to be wrong. Potter was sentenced to two years in prison, despite the prosecutor's demand for more. She deserved no prison time for her honest but tragic mistake.

Potter should appeal her conviction and denial of bail. Not only should police organizations file briefs in her support, so should civil liberties groups like the American Civil Liberties Union, which should be concerned about the misapplication of the criminal law to satisfy voters.

The Minnesota appellate courts should carefully review the record in this case, including the evidence and the judge's instructions. The function of appellate courts is to be a step removed from the passions of the crowd and to apply the law neutrally and fairly. Such an application of the law to Officer Potter should result in an immediate decision to free her on bail, and then a subsequent decision to reverse her conviction, with instructions to dismiss the indictment.

Officer Potter is not a criminal. She did not commit a crime. She appeared devastated by her mistake, both at the time of the incident and when she testified in her own defense. Both justice and the rule of law require that she be set free.

The consequences of unjustly charging, convicting, and imprisoning Kim Potter with the serious crime of manslaughter go well beyond this case, this location, and this time. It reflects a growing danger of weaponizing the criminal justice system in response to the demands of protesters. Our Constitution protects, as it should, the right of every member of the public to protest, to seek justice for victims, and to demand a redress of grievances. But these protests are appropriately directed at legislators, governors, presidents, and other elected officials. They have no place in the proper administration of justice. They certainly should not influence jurors. But nor should they influence prosecutors, even those who are elected. We are the only Western democracy that elects prosecutors, and there is considerable dispute as to whether that is a good idea. But even if it is, elected prosecutors must resist the demands of the crowd to violate the rule of law and seek revenge rather than justice. They failed that test in the Potter case.

D. Kyle Rittenhouse

Kyle Rittenhouse was accused of killing two supporters of Black Lives Matter during a violent demonstration. He was put on trial, however, for two very different offenses. The prosecution accused him of being in the wrong place for the wrong reasons and of carrying a gun to a volatile situation. Rittenhouse's lawyers defended him against a very different charge—namely, that he did not act in self-defense during the moments when he was confronted with a skateboard and a loaded gun. (The prosecution has the burden of proving a negative in self-defense cases.)

Anyone who watched biased commentators on CNN or MSNBC would have focused on the prosecution's charges. Anyone who watched the actual trial live would have understood that the case was far narrower and that the only issue was whether Rittenhouse reasonably feared for his life during the moments before he fired the shots that killed two men and wounded a third.

Had he been tried for the prosecution's version of the crime, I would have judged him morally guilty. He never should have gone to Kenosha. He never should have armed himself. And he never should have gotten into a situation where he might have to use lethal force in self-defense.

But those were not the charges. And, indeed, they could not be the charges, because his actions—morally wrong as they may have been—were protected by the First and Second Amendments to the US Constitution.

Had I been on this jury, I would have found him not guilty because the government failed to prove beyond a reasonable doubt that he did not act in self-defense. His testimony was credible. I believed that his tears were genuine when he testified and again when the verdict was rendered.

Viewers who actually saw his testimony could judge for themselves whether television newscasters and analysts, who in many instances prejudged the case, had correctly characterized his crying as white privileged crocodile tears. That is why live coverage of trials is important: It serves as a check on biased commentators who cheer for certain outcomes and fail to objectively report on the facts. Observers who actually watched the trial were unlikely to be surprised at the outcome. But those who received their information filtered through biased commentators were likely to be shocked.

Had Rittenhouse been convicted, it certainly is possible that his conviction would have been reversed on appeal because the prosecutors committed serious errors. They misinformed the jury about whether an armed man can claim self-defense against an unarmed assailant. (He can, under certain circumstances, as George Zimmerman did.) They withheld from the defense a high-quality version of a crucial video. The double jeopardy prohibition precludes an appeal by the prosecution from a not guilty verdict or a second criminal trial. It does not preclude civil claims, of course, but they, too, are unlikely to succeed, based on the facts.

Kyle Rittenhouse is not a hero and should not be lionized. The last thing we need in this deeply divided nation is armed vigilantes traveling to volatile situations to protect property from rioters. That is the job of trained law enforcement officers, not 17-year-old kids with AR-15 weapons.

But a criminal trial of a particular individual for a specific crime should never be turned into a referendum on racial, social, or political justice. It must focus on the specific facts and law. The verdict is not designed to send a message, or to become a rallying cry for any particular group or ideology. It is only a determination based upon admissible evidence of whether the prosecution has met its heavy burden of proving each of the elements against a defendant.

On the day the jury rendered its verdict of not guilty, New York's resigned governor, Andrew Cuomo, tweeted: "Today's verdict is a stain on the soul of America, & sends a dangerous message about who & what values our justice system was designed to protect. We must stand unified in rejecting supremacist vigilantism & with one voice say: this is not who we are."

I agree that we must reject supremacist vigilantism, but I disagree that this verdict sends a "dangerous message." To the contrary, if anything, it sends a positive message—namely, that jurors are capable of separating facts from ideology and can do justice in an individual case based only on the evidence and the law.

E. The McMichaels

I applauded the convictions of Gregg and Travis McMichael in the killing of the unarmed Ahmaud Arbery but wondered if there was sufficient evidence to convict William Bryan of felony murder, based on his lesser role in the killing. For ideologies, the issue was "all or nothing." They were all guilty, regardless of the evidentiary differences. But the rule of law requires individualized justice, and the appellate courts should scrupulously review the evidence against Bryan to determine whether it establishes beyond a reasonable doubt the crime for which he was convicted. Following the state convictions, the three were convicted of a federal hate crime for the killing.

F. Malik Faisal Akram

It is interesting, though not surprising, that the killing of Malik Faisal Akram—the Muslim man who held hostages in a Texas synagogue, did not create the kind of protests that often follow when law enforcement officers kill a minority person.

Although not all the facts are yet known, the ones we do know raise the troubling question of why the FBI had to kill Akram. This is certainly not a popular question to ask, as we rightfully celebrate the heroic escape of the hostages, but it is an important one. I received significant criticism for raising this question.

Based on what we know, the three remaining hostages—one had been released earlier—had already scurried to safety before the FBI opened fire. If that is true, why didn't the FBI simply leave Akram alone, surrounded in the synagogue and with no hostages for bargaining chips? Did he pose a danger to anyone at that point? He was armed, but a man with a loaded pistol surrounded by dozens of well-protected SWAT team members would not seem to pose a sufficient threat to warrant the use of lethal force when there were non-lethal alternatives. They could simply have waited him out at that point, until he fell asleep or became hungry. It is true that he might have killed himself—he said he would not emerge alive—but that would be no worse than what actually happened.

There may be good explanations for the course of action under-taken by the FBI. Maybe the SWAT team was unsure that all the hostages were safe at the moment when it made its first move. Perhaps the attack began before the hostages escaped. The "fog of war" applies to nighttime rescue operations, as it does in war. There are several related questions that should be asked: Who made the decision to breach the synagogue and go after the hostage-taker? Was it justified at the time it was made? Once the SWAT team was in the synagogue, did they have to use lethal force? Did the hostage-taker fire at them? Did he pose any other threat? These judgment calls had to be made quickly and under pressure. It is easy to Monday morning quarterback any such decision, and we should resist the temptation to do so, while at the same time asking questions that may be import-ant for future hostage situations.

So I am not judging or condemning the FBI. Nor am I defend-ing Akram. What he did was indefensible, and he should have been killed if that were necessary to save the hostages. But was it?

It would have been far better for Akram to be taken alive, ques-tioned, and put on trial, if that could have been done safely. The FBI might have learned about others who may have been complicit, or about other plots. They may also have learned how he was able to get into the US so easily.

But the fundamental issue transcends the benefits and costs of capture versus killing. As a nation, we are involved in a debate—some call it a "reckoning"—about the use of deadly force, especially as directed against racial minorities. Although this is not the typical case of police overreaction, it may bear on the more general issue.

So let all the facts be disclosed and serve as the basis for a discus-sion about the use of deadly force and its alternatives during hostage situations. All reasonable doubts should always be resolved in favor of protecting the hostages and against the hostage-taker. But there will be situations in which there are no such doubts—in which not using deadly force poses no risk to the hostages or the SWAT team. Was this one of those situations? Only a fair and open consideration of all evidence will answer that pressing question.

Taking sides in cases, with little regard for the evidence or law, goes beyond race, religion, and ethnicity. It plagues all sides of the partisan divide. We should focus on principle rather than political, ideological, or identity preferences.

Alex Baldwin's accidental shooting of Halyna Hutchins is another example of how the public chooses sides.

G. Alec Baldwin

The shooting of Halyna Hutchins is first and foremost a tragedy. It should never have happened. It resulted from cost- and corner-cutting. As a caring human being, I extend my warmest condolences to the Hutchins family.

As a criminal law professor for half a century, the case fascinates me. It is one I would have discussed in class and might well have given as an exam question.

In general, ordinary negligence is not a crime. As I have written, Minneapolis police officer Kim Potter's mistake of pulling out the wrong weapon—which resulted in her killing Duante Wright—should never have been charged as a crime. And it wouldn't have been, if not for the George Floyd and other police killings.

So, what about the shooting of Halyna Hutchins? Under New Mexico law, negligent homicide by firing a gun is a petty misdemeanor. For it to rise to the level of a felony requires a higher level of culpability.

There is an easy question of culpability and a hard one in this case. The easy question is whether there is culpability as a general matter of <u>morality</u>. The answer is clearly yes. The killing of Halyna Hutchins may or may not also have been a crime. It was the result of gross negligence and willful decisions by some person or persons to cut corners by hiring inexperienced—and as it turns out, incompetent—professionals, whose job it was to prevent just this sort of tragedy.

The hard question is who, if anybody, is criminally responsible? This may sound like a foolish question—if there was a crime, how can there be doubt about who the criminal is? But there is an enormous difference between concluding that criminal conduct <u>occurred</u> and being able to pinpoint a <u>particular individual</u> against whom guilt can be established beyond a reasonable doubt.

There is no presumption of innocence as to whether a death should be deemed criminal. The presumption of innocence attaches not to events, but to individuals. So, strange as it may seem, there can be a "crime" without there being a "criminal." That may well be the case here.

It will be exceedingly difficult, based on the evidence as we now know it, to prove beyond a reasonable doubt that Alec Baldwin is guilty of a crime. Yes, he had responsibilities as the last actor handling the gun and as one of the producers who oversees the entire enterprise. That may be enough for civil liability, but it will be difficult to prove criminal negligence because the person responsible for handing him the gun assured him that it was "cold."

So, the question then becomes, does the person who handed Baldwin the gun bear criminal responsibility for not checking it? That depends on that person's precise role, and what he or she did or didn't do.

Though several people may be charged together, this crime cannot be charged as a conspiracy, because there was probably no agreement, explicit or implicit, to allow a loaded gun on the set. Rather, the combined actions and inactions of a number of interrelated people brought about the tragedy.

The death of Brandon Lee in 1993 made clear that, when it comes to accidental shootings on movie sets, there is civil responsibility, and increased the likelihood that one or more people would be charged with a crime in the event of future shootings on future film sets. But the more recent case is not a slam dunk under New Mexico law. Nor would it be under the laws of most other jurisdictions.

The key question remains: how do we prevent this kind of utterly preventable tragedy from ever occurring again? I played an advisory role in the Brandon Lee case, and I thought its result—no criminal prosecution, but considerable civil liability—would change the realities on every movie set. That didn't happen, as evidenced by this tragedy. Will it now happen? Or will profits still be placed before safety?

There is one simple and obvious solution. Laws must be passed absolutely prohibiting the presence of any fireable weapon or any projectile capable of being fired from a weapon on any movie set. The Second Amendment is not for movie sets. Real guns have no place in the hands of actors. CGI technology has improved immeasurably since the Brandon Lee case. The firing of every gun in every movie must be filmed using CGI rather than gunpowder, blanks, or real guns. This should have been done immediately following the Brandon Lee case. It must be done now. No questions asked. Life is more important than making movies or saving a few dollars.

Let the preventable death of Halyna Hutchins serve to prevent future deaths on movie sets.

H. Ghislaine Maxwell

Ghislaine Maxwell was also subjected to two different trials with two different sets of witnesses. One was in the courtroom and the other on the courthouse steps and in the media.

The trial in the courtroom accused her essentially of grooming underage females for sexual abuse by Jeffrey Epstein. The trial in the media accused her of helping Jeffrey Epstein traffic two adult women—Virginia Giuffre and Sarah Ransome—to numerous prominent men and women.

It is the second trial that has garnered the most media attention because Giuffre has accused Prince Andrew, Senator George Mitchell, Ambassador Bill Richardson, Prime Minister Ehud Barak, billionaire Leslie Wexner, Professor Marvin Minsky, real estate mogul Tom Pritzker, hedge fund operator Glenn Dubin, Jacques Cousteau's granddaughter Alexandra—and me. Ransome has named Donald Trump, Hillary Clinton, Richard Branson—and me. These media accusers made the most serious and detailed accusations against Maxwell and Epstein, both under oath and in the media. The obvious questions arise therefore: Why did the government not use them as witnesses against Maxwell and why were they not included in the original indictment against Epstein? Why did the government not call "Maxwell's most prominent accusers" who are at the "forefront of the case?" Why are such central players "conspicuously absent from the witness list?" Why did the government leave such a "gaping hole that the jurors may find unsettling?" Why "this empty chair?"

These obvious questions are being asked by some media and legal experts many of whom know the answer but refuse to provide it. The answer should be obvious to anyone familiar with the facts: The government did not call Virginia Giuffre because they don't believe she is credible and because, according to the testimony of a witness who they do believe, she herself was complicit in Maxwell's alleged crimes.

The rest of the media should be asking these critical questions. The answers should be clear, to anyone who examines the evidence.

Virginia Giuffre's own lawyers have disputed her accounts in recorded statements as I have documented. In a TV interview, Bradley Edwards has said that based on his 11-year investigation, he does not believe that "any high-profile people would be implicated;" he also said that Leslie Wexner did not participate in any sexual activities with Giuffre. In other words, he has essentially called Giuffre a perjurer since she swore under oath that she had sex on multiple occasions with prominent people including Wexner. Giuffre's other lawyer, David Boies, said in a recorded conversation with me that my travel and other records convinced him that it would have been "impossible" for her to have had sexual or any contact with me during the relevant time period, and that she was simply "wrong" in accusing me. Her own emails and writing establish that I never even met her, as she herself admitted when she tried to sell her memoir.

Had Giuffre been called as a witness, the government would have been obliged under the Brady rule to have provided all this information—and more—to the defense. I know the government has this material because I gave it to them! But even if the government provided this information to the defense, they would have been precluded from calling Giuffre as a witness and vouching for her credibility, because they know she is not credible.

The other reason the government didn't call her is that a government witness at Maxwell's trial named Carolyn Andriano testified that she was trafficked to Jeffrey Epstein by Virginia Giuffre when she was 14. Giuffre was above the age of consent when she sold Carolyn to Epstein for cash. According to Carolyn's testimony, Giuffre started to groom her when she was a 13-year-old elementary school student. Giuffre would pick her up from school and smoke pot with her. "I trusted her," Carolyn said.

When Carolyn turned 14, Giuffre decided that she was ready to be trafficked to Epstein, so she told her to dress sexy and lie about her age if asked. Giuffre then picked Carolyn up in her car and drove her to Epstein's house. She took her to Epstein's massage room, where Giuffre proceeded to get naked and have sex with Epstein: she "climbed on top of him and proceeded to have sex with him." She had sex with Epstein in front of the 14-year-old, obviously to encourage her to do the same. It worked. Carolyn then began a sexual relationship with Epstein that lasted for several years. In payment for performing this trafficking service, Giuffre was paid in cash. The government, in using Carolyn but not Giuffre as a witness in the Maxwell case, vouched for Carolyn's credibility but not for Giuffre's.

Carolyn has since said that Giuffre wasn't coerced into trafficking her: "I don't think she was coerced into doing anything." She volunteered to do if for money. Epstein didn't ask her to bring Carolyn. He didn't even know she existed. Giuffre understood that she would be paid handsomely for bringing any underage girl to Epstein.

These facts are essentially undisputed. Giuffre herself has admitted bringing underage girls to Epstein, knowing what he would do to them. Her lawyer, David Boies, has acknowledged "her role in facilitating other young women's involvement." Giuffre now claims she did it because she was afraid of Epstein, but the evidence is to the contrary. Giuffre had her own apartment, car, and money. She was free to leave at any time, which she did on several occasions.

Giuffre wasn't compelled to groom and traffic Carolyn. It was her voluntary decision as an adult to traffic her for money. She was old enough to vote, serve in the army, and commit felonies. She was certainly old enough to know that she was guilty of recruiting underage girls as a part of a pyramid scheme from which she bene-fitted financially. As Carolyn put it: "I don't think Virginia deserves anything less than what Maxwell is getting because she trafficked me." Giuffre now claims under oath that she has "no recollection of this individual." This is probably because she trafficked so many children that it is difficult for her to distinguish one trafficked "indi-vidual" child from the others.

Perhaps Giuffre was once a victim of Epstein, though Carolyn insists she was "pretty cool" and not "upset" about allegedly getting to have sex with Prince Andrew: "I got to sleep with him!" she bragged. But victims, too, can become victimizers. And law enforcement should investigate whether Giuffre victimized Carolyn and the other underage girls she recruited and trafficked. They should also investigate whether she is now victimizing those she has accused of having sex with her.

A one-time victim—if Giuffre is even that—is not above the law. She was an adult when she trafficked a 14-year-old. She was a wealthy middle-aged woman when she committed perjury against me and possibly others. She should be treated as a responsible adult, not infantilized as a permanent victim.

Now at age 38, Giuffre is anything but a helpless victim. She is an eight-figure multimillionaire. She just bought one of the most expensive houses in Western Australia. She is represented by some of the most prominent law firms in America.

Virtually every penny Giuffre has made has been from sex: first she was paid for having sex with Epstein, and she claims with oth-ers. For example, she said she was paid $15,000 in cash for having sex with Prince Andrew. When she was too old for Epstein, she was paid for trafficking underage children to him. Then, in her 30s, she was paid hush money to settle lawsuits (David Boies said in a conversation recorded before she filed her lawsuits that if she was paid millions of dollars she would go back to Australia and never write a book or give interviews—so much for being an advocate for victims!).

Now she has obtained a reported multi-million dollar settlement from Prince Andrew for voluntarily having paid sex with him ("I got to sleep with him," it was "pretty cool"). She has admitted that she didn't pay taxes on her earlier illicit earnings, and it is unclear when she started paying taxes on her recent windfalls.

In order for Giuffre to testify, she would have to be given immunity from prosecution for her own crimes, committed for money as an adult. That would have made her a terrible witness.

Thus, the real reason why Giuffre isn't being called are obvious. But her lawyer and the media are obscuring the truth. David Boies told the *Miami Herald* that he was "mystified" by their decision, but it probably related to the fact that they are only "bringing charges with women who were under the age of consent at the time." But Giuffre initially swore she was 15 when she first had sex with Epstein and Maxwell. She vividly remembered spending her "sweet 16 birthday" with them. The age of consent in Florida is 18. When confronted with employment records, she changed her testimony and said she was 16—still below the age of consent. (Other records suggest she was 17, above the age of consent in New York and Great Britain.) Moreover, one of the alleged victims—Kate, who was called as a government witness—was well above the age of consent. So Boies's argument is nonsense.

The writer of the *Miami Herald* article about why Giuffre was not called, Julie Brown, knows that the real reason is Giuffre's lack of credibility. I gave Brown the above information about Giuffre. But Brown had relied on Giuffre as a major source for her prize-winning articles about Epstein and Maxwell. To acknowledge Giuffre's lack of credibility now would undercut the credibility of the articles. So Brown has provided other implausible excuses, such as the age of consent—omitting to report the fact that it is 18 in Florida.

There is nothing mystifying about the government's decision not to call Giuffre: They don't believe her. Her lawyers don't believe her. Her friends don't believe her. And neither should anyone else. What is mystifying is why the media won't honestly report on this important development. The answer is that most of the media is committed to certain narratives, and they refuse to investigate or report on facts that undercut their narrative.

Sarah Ransome, who was outside the courtroom on the first day of the trial and who has written a book, has admitted to the *New Yorker* that she made up fantastic stories about having sex tapes of Hillary Clinton, Donald Trump, Richard Branson, and others. During the 2016 election, she sent dozens of emails to Maureen Callahan of the *New York Post* demanding that they publish stories, about these "pedophiles" and the sex tapes. But she then admitted to the *New Yorker* that she had no such tapes and that she had made up the stories entirely in order to have something over Epstein.

If Giuffre and Ransome had been telling the truth, they would be the most incriminating witnesses against Maxwell. It is they who claim they were trafficked to Epstein associates. But the government is obviously aware of the above evidence that destroys their credibility. So, they carefully crafted the indictment against Maxwell (and the previous one against Epstein) to avoid using these women as witnesses. It is unethical for a prosecutor to rely on witnesses who they know or believe lack credibility.

But the media has no such constraints. Most media have simply continued to present Giuffre and Ransome as credible witnesses, without reporting on the incontrovertible evidence—including their own lawyers' statements and their own writings and admissions—that prove that these witnesses have histories of making false accusations. Journalists seem unwilling to challenge the credibility of "victims," lest they be accused of "victim shaming." They refuse to recognize the nuanced truth that a woman can be both a victim of Epstein and a victimizer of his associates (see Chapter 11).

The trial of Ghislaine Maxwell inside the courtroom did not disclose this complex reality. That is not its proper function. It is the role of the media to investigate, with equal resources, the credibility of both accused and accusers. Thus far, it has failed in this important duty. It's not too late. The evidence is available. All that is required is the courage to pursue uncomfortable and unpopular truths.

I. The Case Against Prince Andrew

Prince Andrew is among the men Virginia Giuffre was accused of having had sex with her when she was over the age of consent and claims she was paid $15,000.

The accusation has ruined his life, his work, and his reputation. He has been stripped of his titles and responsibilities based on this accusation.

But what if his accuser, Virginia Giuffre, simply made up the story? What if she, in fact, only posed for a photograph with Prince Andrew, and then used that "evidence" to falsely claim that she had sex with him? What if she framed Prince Andrew in order to obtain another mega-settlement?

What if Prince Andrew is actually innocent?

I am not asking the readers of this article to believe Prince Andrew in his denials of ever having had sex with the accuser. None of us knows what happened or didn't happen after that photograph was taken. I am only asking the reader to *assume*, simply for purposes of analysis, the possibility that Prince Andrew *might* be innocent.

As soon as Giuffre accused him, he was presumed guilty. If he had been charged by an official government agency, say a prosecutor or grand jury, he would be presumed innocent as a matter of law, even though the imprimatur of the government was behind the accusation.

Here, no governmental agency or unbiased official has ever accused Prince Andrew of a crime. His only accuser is an individual who stood to benefit financially from the accusation. Yet the media and public opinion seem to presume Prince Andrew is guilty.

The *New York Times* reports that there "are legal charges hanging over him." This suggests that some unbiased institution has leveled charges. But anyone can be sued by anyone—hence the expression, "The Pope can be sued for paternity."

A lawsuit for money brought by an individual should never give rise to any kind of presumption of guilt. As Judge Jose A. Cabranes of the US Court of Appeals has cautioned the media and the public:

> Materials submitted by parties to a court should be understood for what they are. They do not reflect the court's own findings. Rather, they are prepared by parties seeking to advance their own interests in an adversarial process. Although affidavits and depositions are

offered "under penalty of perjury," it is in fact exceedingly rare for anyone to be prosecuted for perjury in a civil proceeding. . . .

Thus, although the act of filing a document with a court might be thought to lend that document additional credibility in fact, allegations appearing in such documents *might be less credible* than those published elsewhere.

[T]he media does the public a profound disservice when it reports on parties' allegations uncritically. . . . Even ordinary critical readers may take the reference to "court papers" as some sort of marker of reliability. *This would be a mistake.* (Emphasis added.)

We therefore urge the media to exercise restraint in covering potentially defamatory allegations, and we caution the public to read such accounts with discernment.

Many in the media have not heeded this wise warning for a number of reasons. One reason could be that media companies profit from reporting salacious accusations against prominent people.

The judge in the Prince Andrew case made it clear that in allowing the case to go forward, he was not deciding who is telling the truth; that would be up to a jury. He was merely assuming, as the law says he must, that the allegations contained in the complaint are true for purposes of further review of evidence.

Yet, the media persists in reporting on the case as if there had been a finding of guilt.

So the fundamental question remains: Why should one individual, with a history of false accusations, have the power to destroy lives, careers, and reputations, based solely on an accusation?

What if the presumption of guilt that seems to have been imposed on Prince Andrew were imposed on all people who were subject to private, adversarial lawsuits? What if it were your brother, sister, or father who was being sued by an individual with a history of falsely accusing people?

Now that Prince Andrew has settled the case, many ask why he would pay so much money if he were innocent of her accusations. He had strong defenses—both legal and factual—against Virginia Giuffre's claim that he sexually assaulted her when she was 17. The technical legal defenses included that she lied when she claimed she was a resident of Colorado, not Australia, when she filed her suit. If so, the federal court lacked diversity jurisdiction and had to dismiss her case. Also, there was the agreement between Giuffre and Epstein, which seems to bar suits against anyone who could have sued at the time. Then there is the possible unconstitutionality of the statute of limitations, which was temporarily expanded to permit a 20-year-old allegation to be resurrected. Finally, there is the reality that Giuffre was above the age of consent and there is no evidence that the prince forced her or that he believed that Epstein had forced her to have sex with him.

The factual defenses are even stronger than the legal ones. I have no idea what happened—or didn't happen—between Prince Andrew and Virginia Giuffre. Neither Jeffrey Epstein nor Ghislaine Maxwell ever discussed the prince with me. But there is a non-original photograph which, if authentic, would establish that they met, in the presence of Maxwell, on at least one occasion. (Maxwell had emailed me in 2015 that "it looks real. I think it is." But her hearsay opinion would not be admissible at a trial.)

Whether they had sex depends completely on the credibility, or lack thereof, of Virginia Giuffre, who I know with 100 percent certainty is not telling the truth about having sex with me. Her own lawyers have acknowledged that I could not have been in the locations where she wrongly claimed to have met me during the relevant time period. That doesn't necessarily mean that she is lying about the prince, but it is relevant to that issue. So is Giuffre's own history of trafficking children to Jeffrey Epstein. And the only corroboration of Giuffre's story comes from Carolyn Andriano, the woman who, at age 14, was trafficked by Giuffre to Epstein.

If Giuffre received many millions of dollars for getting to sleep with the prince when she was an adult, imagine how much more Andriano might get if she sued Giuffre for trafficking her to Epstein when she was a child!

If I had been the prince's lawyer, I would have called Andriano as a witness. Yes, she would testify that Giuffre told her "She got to sleep with" Andrew, but she would also testify that Giuffre bragged about what a cool thing it was. Also, her testimony about being trafficked by Giuffre would show that Giuffre's reputation as an opponent of child trafficking is questionable.

So, why did he settle? Because he (or the Queen) didn't want the prince to be deposed. Depositions are open-ended and not constrained by rigorous rules of evidence. He could have been asked about his reputation—deserved or undeserved—as "Randy Andy." He could have been questioned about his sexual history in general, not limited to Giuffre's specific allegations.

Once the judge ruled that the prince had to submit to a deposition, the pressure to settle became unbearable, and to avoid the humiliation of a deposition, he agreed to pay her off without admitting any guilt.

The threat of being deposed only works on people who have something to hide. That is why I have willingly submitted to depositions and eagerly await a trial at which the whole truth—about my history and Giuffre's—will be presented to a jury and made public. She is trying to get money from me, but I will never pay her one penny for dropping her false accusations against me, because I have nothing to hide.

These are issues that need to be debated, but today's media seems less interested in discussing complex moral and legal issues than in assuming the worst about public figures.

In all of these cases, the race, gender, celebrity, and "face" of the accused and the alleged victim play a role—more of a role than principle and evidence—in attitudes toward the appropriate outcome. This is not as it should be. The blindfold must be placed back on the statue—and the reality—of justice, if we are to remain a nation governed by the rule of law.

Principle must govern not only criminal cases but also constitutional cases involving large issues such as abortion and gun control. Decisions in the cases, too, must satisfy the shoe on the other foot principle.

J. Abortion, Gun Control, and Court Packing
Abortion and gun control are two of the most controversial issues in our nation. The Supreme Court has ruled that most abortions are

protected by the Constitution and that most private gun ownership is likewise protected. *Roe v. Wade* was decided by a 7–2 vote of the court's justices; *Heller v. District of Columbia* by a 5–4 vote.

Now, Texas has devised a mechanism for effectively outlawing nearly all abortions by offering a $10,000 bounty to any citizen who sues an abortion provider or anyone else who aids or abets a girl or woman in obtaining an abortion after a heartbeat is detected in the fetus. This generally occurs at about six weeks into the pregnancy, when some females who are pregnant don't yet realize it.

The Texas lawmakers who enacted the end run around *Roe* understand that under current Supreme Court precedent, a six-week pregnant girl or woman has an absolute constitutional right to an abortion. If the state had merely outlawed all such abortions—made providers and facilitators subject to criminal penalties—the Supreme Court might well strike down such a direct affront to *Roe*. (A Mississippi law which prohibits most abortions after about 15 weeks is now before the high court.) So, instead, Texas seeks to deter those who would facilitate abortions after six weeks by threatening them with a civil lawsuit, brought not by the state but by private citizens.

This tactic has produced an initial victory from five justices who refused to enjoin the law. Accordingly, many Texas abortion providers, fearful of being sued, have stopped their constitutionally protected activities, just as the Texas lawmakers hoped they would.

The Department of Justice and abortion rights advocates are now scrambling to devise responses to this new, and thus far, effective method for ending most abortions. Some highly technical proposals seem unlikely to persuade the five justices. Others—such as criminally prosecuting, in federal court, anyone who sues under the law—raise serious civil liberties issues: Obeying a state law, even one that may be held unconstitutional later but which the Supreme Court has refused to enjoin, may violate due process.

There is, however, another response—a political one—that fights fire with fire and may at least make other states think hard about following Texas's lead. It also may give pause to the five conservative

justices before they consider approving the Texas end run around
Roe.

Following the enactment of the Texas bounty law, I published the
following out-of-the-box proposal: Liberal, pro-gun-control states
could apply the Texas bounty approach to gun control. New York or
Illinois, for example, could declare that gun crime has gotten so serious that the private ownership of most handguns should be deterred.
It would be unconstitutional for the state to authorize the criminal
prosecution of those who facilitate constitutionally protected gun
ownership. But the state could, instead, enact a gun-bounty civil law
modeled on the Texas abortion law. It would empower any citizen
to sue for $10,000 anyone who facilitates the sale or ownership of
handguns.

Gun ownership advocates would rail against such a law as circumventing *Heller*, just as abortion advocates are railing against the
Texas law as circumventing *Roe*. But it would be hard for the courts
to uphold the civil mechanism of the anti-abortion law without also
upholding the identical mechanism in the anti-gun law.

Creating this "shoe on the other foot" challenge would bring
home the dangerous implications of the Texas bounty approach
which, if not stopped, could undercut the authority of the Supreme
Court to enforce other constitutional rights. Texas could, for example, next apply it to gay marriage—any private citizen could sue
anyone who performed or facilitated same-sex marriages—thus circumventing *Obergefell v. Hodges*. New York could then apply it to
Citizens United v. FCC and offer a civil bounty to sue any media out-
let that ran corporate political ads. Any state could simply target any
Supreme Court precedent it doesn't like and deter its enforcement
by authorizing citizens who oppose it to sue. This would empower
every state to effectively overrule Supreme Court decisions, as some
southern states unsuccessfully tried to do following *Brown v Board of
Education* in 1954.

The downside of this "what's good for the goose" approach is
that it requires state legislators to enact statutes that they may
well believe are unconstitutional. Two constitutional wrongs do
not a constitutional right make. But the Supreme Court's decision

to allow the Texas statute to be enforced, at least for now, can be seen as a green light for other states to follow suit, at least until the high court were to rule on the constitutionality of the Texas bounty tactic. Indeed, California and New York have proposed laws that would empower citizens to bring civil suits against some gun sellers. So stay tuned.

This is far from a perfect solution to a very imperfect and dangerous tactic concocted by Texas. But it will make those who devised it understand that they have created a monster that can easily be turned against rights that they cherish.

The issue would be mooted if the Supreme Court were to overrule *Roe v. Wade* and permit every state to ban all or most abortions.

Overruling or severally limiting *Roe v. Wade* would widely be viewed as an unprincipled act of partisan power as distinguished from a proper exercise in legal judgment. This fear was expressed by liberal members of the courts minority and is almost certainly of deep concern to Chief Justice John Roberts. The High Court's standing in polls has dropped considerably since its transparently partisan decision in *Bush v. Gore* more than 20 years ago. Since that time, it has rendered controversial decisions both increasing and undercutting fundamental rights such as gay marriage, and religious freedom. It has also dramatically expanded gun rights. During this period, the pendulum has swung quite narrowly. Justices appointed by Republican presidents have occasionally voted with those appointed by Democratic presidents and vice versa.

This seems to be changing with the appointments of three justices in four years by former President Donald Trump who was open about trying to reshape the court along party lines. The influence of appointing an individual justice was manifested most clearly by the debacle over the failed appointment of Merrick Garland by President Obama and the successful appointment of Amy Coney Barrett in the run up to the 2020 election. The forthcoming decision on abortion rights will surely reflect those events as well as President Trump's two earlier appointments.

The fear that the Supreme Court has become a political institution indistinguishable from the two elected branches of government is partly accurate. The truth is more nuanced. The court is less likely to be partisan in the majority of its cases that represent important but largely noncontroversial legal issues, such as resolving conflicts among the circuits over statutory construction and the like. These cases form a substantial part of the court's docket. But several deeply controversial and high-profile cases are on every year's docket, and it is these cases that are often influenced by partisan appointments. That is not always the case, as evidenced by the unanimous decision—that included two Clinton appointees—back in 1998 compelling President Bill Clinton to submit to depositions in a civil case. But just two years later, the court's 5–4 decision ending Al Gore's run for the presidency was transparently partisan.

So, the makeup of the docket determines how partisan and political the decisions are likely to be. This is significant because the justices determine their own docket: it takes four votes to grant review. Justice Louis Brandeis once observed that the most important decisions made by the justices are deciding not to take a case. The corollary is that a discretionary decision to take a case, as was made in the recent Mississippi abortion case, can be highly partisan and have profound consequences.

Were a divided decision along partisan lines to be rendered overruling or severely limiting *Roe*, the Court would become a primary battlefield in the cultural wars that divide our nation. But some will argue that these wars began with *Roe v. Wade*, and it was inevitable that each side would seek victory through partisan appointments. There may be some truth to this, but there is also truth to the argument that it is better to develop a right, such as the right of privacy, over many years, as was done with regard to *Roe*, than to abrogate it based entirely on a change in the makeup of the court.

This is not the first time such an abrupt change occurred. When Franklin Delano Roosevelt threatened to pack the court so that his New Deal would be held constitutional, shifts occurred that upheld most of the New Deal. Historians have called it "the switch in time that saved nine." As several justices who seem to want to overrule *Roe* have observed, the court has on occasion overruled precedents of long duration, such as *Plessy v. Ferguson* which authorized segregation and the cases that refused to recognize gay rights. Most of these decisions, however, expanded constitutional rights. Overruling *Roe* would contract a woman's right to choose. Critics of *Roe* point out that it would expand the fetus' right to life. That is why this decision, unlike the gay rights and gay marriage decision, involves a clash of rights, at least for those who believe that life begins at conception or shortly thereafter. Gay rights and gay marriage on the other hand involve no such clash. No one has a legitimate right to prevent people from making sexual and marital choices that do not involve other people.

Overruling or severely limiting *Roe* would be the worst instance of partisan power politics by the justices. To be sure, the five Republicans who voted to end the recount in 2000 were engaging in pure partisan politics. But at least they had the justification— perhaps excuse is a better word—that there was an emergency. As Justice Antonin Scalia wrote to me in response to my criticism of the decision: "Even if you think that [I] was wrong, considering the severe time constraint [and] the pressure to come out with a near unanimous opinion . . . you should cut me some slack. . . . We will talk about it sometime, as you say, before senility."

The Mississippi case poses no comparable emergency. Review need not have been granted; *Roe* has been on the books for half a century. it should remain the law of the land.

But what if the justices decide to overrule or severely limit *Roe*? Will the Democrats respond by packing the court with liberal justices who will restore *Roe*?

The commission appointed by President Biden to assess his options with regard to the Supreme Court released a report that made no specific recommendations but several of its members have advocated packing the court to achieve a liberal majority. This move is likely to garner more support if the high court were to overrule *Roe v. Wade*, which the recent oral arguments in the Mississippi case suggests it might do.

Were the Democrats to pack the currently conversative Supreme Court with a majority of liberals, you can be sure the Republicans would play tit for tat when they take control over the other two branches.

They will pack the court with more conservative justices. And then the Democrats would add even more when they come to power.

What would then become of the Supreme Court? And what would become of a woman's right to choose abortion?

No one can know for certain, but the likely outcome would be an even more politicized and partisan high court than we currently have. Proponents of court packing will argue that the Republicans have already "packed" this court by refusing to confirm President Obama's nominee, Merrick Garland, and then confirming President Trump's nominee, Justice Amy Coney Barrett on the eve of the 2020 election. Her seat legitimately belongs to the Democrats, and it was stolen from them. They may well be correct, but that does not justify a systemic change in the Supreme Court that would alter the nature of that institution forever, turning it into a court whose composition would change with every political shift in power.

As Nancy Gertner, a former federal judge, tried to make the case for packing: The Republicans have "manipulated its membership" and "whatever the cost of expansion in the short run, I believe will be more than counterbalanced by the real benefits to judicial independence and to our democracy." But she got it exactly backwards: There might be benefits in the short run, but in the long run, it would undermine judicial independence and the rule of law by turning the Supreme Court into an unstable institution, whose membership would consistently be expanded to meet the short term needs of the party in power.

Packing the court to preserve a woman's right to choose would also turn that important right into a political football whose content would vary with the political trends. Today she would have that right; tomorrow she wouldn't, and the day after tomorrow there would be uncertainty.

Most fundamentally, court packing would weaken our Constitution, our system of checks and balances, and the rule of law. Proponents of court packing will argue that these evils have already occurred due to the actions of the Republicans. But court packing would exacerbate them and make them more enduring.

What then should Democrats do to preserve a woman's right to choose and other fundamental rights that are at risk from the current conservative majority? They should try to use their legislative and executive power, rather than diminish the power of the judicial branch. They should get Congress to pass a national right to choose law that legislates the right under the commerce clause. Abortion is an issue that goes beyond the borders of any particular state. Many women and girls who are denied an abortion in Mississippi or Texas will travel to more permissive states, thus burdening their clinics and hospitals. I believe Congress has the constitutional power to legislate a national right to choose, though it is far from certain that this Supreme Court would uphold such an exercise of commerce clause power.

Nor is it certain that the Democrats have enough senate votes to enact such a law. But lack of certainty is not a good enough reason to endanger the credibility and authority of the Supreme Court—an institution that has served the nation well over time, despite its many questionable and some terrible decisions. It may be broke, but the fix of court packing is more dangerous than leaving it as it is.

Some repairs, however, may well be in order. Lifetime tenure for judges is a mistake. There ought to be term limits—say 15 to 20 years. Only kings, queens, and popes should serve for life. Age limitations—say 70—would be a mistake, because it would encourage president to nominate younger and younger justices. Justices Holmes, Brandeis, and Ginsburg, among others, were 60 when they were nominated, and they served with distinction for decades.

So, packing the court as a short-term response to this current conservative bent may backfire. Over the long term, a stable court will do more to preserve important rights than an unstable court, whose members would shift with the political winds.

More fundamentally, a Supreme Court that rendered all decisions on enduring constitutional <u>principles</u>, rather than on partisan advantage would be best for the rule of law and our system of checks and balances.

For the most part, the judiciary has been the most principled and least partisan branch. Its principled neutrality is now in danger of being compromised by partisan extremists. All Americans will benefit if this danger is averted.

CHAPTER 7

Unprincipled Attacks on Israel

_____

Israel is subject to more unprincipled attacks than any other country of comparable size. There are principled criticisms as well as there should be of any nation. Israelis themselves are a critical people and its media is hyper-critical of many of its policies and leaders. As Tom Friedman, a Pulitzer Prize winning columnist for the *New York Times* so aptly put it: "Criticizing Israel is not anti-Semitic and saying so is vile. But singling out Israel for opprobrium and international sanction out of all proportion to any other party in the Middle East is anti-Semitic, and not saying so is dishonest."

A perfect example of the double standard applied to Israel is the boycott movement singling out the nation state of the Jewish people—BDS. The godfather of this bigoted tactic was the late Bishop Desmond Tutu. Recently the Ben and Jerry ice cream company and its corporate owner Unilever decided to join that campaign against Israel.

Bennett Cohen and Jerry Greenfield have tried to defend the decision to boycott the West Bank and other disputed territories in Israel. But their self-serving defense fails to put their namesake ice cream company's actions in a proper context. Both Ben & Jerry's ice cream and its corporate owner, Unilever, continue to sell their products in many of the most repressive countries in the world—countries that murder dissidents, imprison journalists, prosecute gays, enslave women, exploit children, and occupy other people's land.

So, the question that Ben and Jerry refuse to answer is: Why do you single out only parts of Israel and Palestinian territories for a boycott? Why not list all the countries in the world that the company serves in order of the seriousness of their human rights violations and boycott them in order of their seriousness?

Such an action would, of course, damage the bottom line of both companies far more than its selective boycott of portions of Israel and the disputed territories.

The issue is not whether one agrees or disagrees with Israeli policies; I disagree with some, just as I disagree with some American policies. The key question is whether singling out part of the nation-state of the Jewish people for a boycott is moral, legal, and proper. Or to put it in more classic terms: "Why the Jews?" A joke from Germany in the 1930s makes the point: Hitler was railing against the Jews and rhetorically asked his audience, "Who is causing all of Germany's problems?" As expected, most of the audience shouted, "The Jews!" But one lonely voice said, "The bicycle riders." Hitler turned to the man who said that and shouted, "Why the bicycle rider?" To which the man replied, "Why the Jews?" Today's voice of principle should ask, "Why the Jewish State?"

The reality is that no country in the Middle East, or indeed in the world today, that is faced with threats comparable to those faced by Israel can boast a better record of human rights, compliance with the rule of law, and concern for the lives of enemy civilians. Israel's record is far from perfect, but it is better than most and better than any other country in the Middle East. Yet, Ben & Jerry's and its parent company continue to sell to other countries in the Middle East and around the world with far worse records. When asked why, they responded that they weren't sure and would look into it. But the bigoted boycott remains.

Nor can this selective boycott be justified on the claim that Israel is different because of its close relation to the United States. Jordan and Egypt receive massive economic and military aid from the United States and have far worse human rights records. The same is true of other recipients of American economic and military aid. The American connection is a phony excuse for bigotry and anti-Semitism against the world's only Jewish state.

Israel's continuing control over the disputed territory is largely a function of Palestinian refusal to accept generous Israeli offers to end the military occupation that began in 1967. Under international law, military occupations are justified so long as resistance continues and peace is not accepted. Israel offered to end its occupation in 2000 and 2001, and again in 2008. It unilaterally ended its occupation of the Gaza Strip in 2005, removing every single soldier and settler.

The result was a Hamas takeover, thousands of rockets, terror tunnels, and continued belligerence. Israel would have every right under international law to reoccupy the Gaza Strip, but it has chosen not to. Were it to abandon its military control over the West Bank without a permanent agreement—which the Palestinians have rejected—it would be inviting a repeat of the Gaza experience, but a much more dangerous one because of the proximity of parts of the West Bank to parts of Israeli population centers and its international airport.

The issues surrounding the continued occupation of the disputed territories, including East Jerusalem and the Jewish Quarter of Jerusalem, including the Western Wall, are complex and difficult. They are not the sort of issues that should give rise to boycotts and other economic sanctions. They are not like the imprisonment of journalists and dissidents by Turkey, not like the gender discrimination practiced by most Arab and Muslim states, not like the detention camps created for Uyghurs by China, not like the denial of basic liberties by Cuba, and certainly not like the hanging of gays by Iranian and Hamas mullahs. Nor is it anything like systemic apartheid practiced by South Africa before Nelson Mandela. Yet, Peter Beinart, a religious Jew who has become Israel's most strident academic enemy, has compared Israel's continuing control over the West Bank and Golan Heights to Russia's unprovoked attack on Ukraine and its deliberate targeting of civilians.

As an advocate for the two-state solution since 1970, I fervently hope that the Israeli government and the Palestinian leadership will return to the negotiating table. But a boycott of the West Bank—which will hurt Palestinians that work for Ben & Jerry's—will not help achieve a two-state solution. Nor will false comparisions to Russia's attempt to conquer Ukraine.

Ben Cohen and Jerry Greenfield, Vermont Jews say they are "supporters of the state of Israel," as contrasted with Beinart who has called for the end of Israel as the nation of the Jewish people. They should all be ashamed of their hypocrisy. I for one will never eat Ben & Jerry's ice cream again, not only because it has too many calories, too much fat, and uses sugar and cocoa from countries that exploit child labor, but because their decision to single out parts of Israel for an economic boycott is anti-Semitic.

Ben & Jerry's Ice Cream is not the only institution that applies an unprincipled double standard to the nation state of the Jewish People. The *New York Times* had a long and sordid history in this regard. A recent episode is only one of many.

In purporting to "report"—not editorialize—about why Congresswoman Alexandria Ocasio-Cortez (AOC) changed her vote from "no" to "present" on the Iron Dome funding, the *New York Times* congressional correspondent Catie Edmonson "reported" the following:

> [Progressives] have been caught between their principles and the still powerful pro-Israel voices in their party, such as influential lobbyists and rabbis.

She cited no support for her "reporting" on the pressure placed by "powerful . . . rabbis," nor did she name them. Her "reporting" simply was not true. She just made it up, because it supported the anti-Semitic narrative that AOC and her "Squad" deploy to deflect justified criticism of their anti-Israel and anti-American votes.

No powerful rabbis or lobbyists were needed to pressure the nearly 500 Democrats and Republicans who voted to fund the Iron Dome defense system that was jointly developed by the United States and Israel and that is currently being used to defend American troops from rocket attacks. The Iron Dome kills no one. It saves the lives of Israeli Jews, Muslims, and Christians who are targeted by Hamas rockets. It also saves the lives of Gaza residents by reducing the need for Israel to invade in order to stop the rockets. No objective person should oppose funding for this lifesaving system. But Edmondson decided to "report"—make up—a canard that has deep roots in the sordid history of anti-Semitism: namely, that powerful rabbis—sometimes called "the elders of Zion"—pressured elected officials to surrender their patriotic American "principles" by voting in an unprincipled way in support of a foreign power. This not only demeans Jews as having dual loyalty, but it also insults every member of Congress who voted for this allegedly "unprincipled" result, presumably because of illicit pressure from lobbyists and rabbis, and not because they believed it was the right thing to do for America and its ally. No mention was made by the *Times* of powerful pro-Palestinian lobbyists or imams, or of the pressure placed on AOC and others by radical leftists who hate Israel. No, it was supposedly "principles" that motivated the anti-Israel votes, and "powerful" rabbinical pressures that determined the "yes" and "present" votes. And this purports to be objective "reporting" from the newspaper of record.

After much criticism, the *Times* quietly removed the reference to "rabbis" without apologizing for its reporter's mendacious anti-Semitism or disciplining her for her journalistic malpractice. Just imagine how quickly a journalist would be cancelled if she engaged in comparable bigotry toward another group. But the *Times* has long suffered from a double standard toward Jews and the Jewish nation.

The *Times* has repeatedly felt the need to apologize for its persistent insensitivity—and worse—toward Israel and its Jewish supporters. Remember the Der Stürmer-like cartoon it published in its international edition, showing the Prime Minister of Israel, portrayed as a seeing eye dog, leading the blind President of the US? It must do better. It must take steps to identify and control biased reporters, such as Edmondson, and reporting, such as her false claim about powerful rabbis, <u>before</u> they have to apologize for the damage that has already been done.

The *Times* has the right to editorialize against Israel, as it constantly does. It has the right to publish multiple columns and op-eds that are skewed against Israel, while employing only one pro-Israel columnist. But it has no journalistic right to editorialize on its *news pages*, as it repeatedly does. It defrauds its readers by disguising its subjective and biased opinions as objective unbiased reporting of the news. In this regard the *Times* is among the worst offenders of any influential newspaper.

So let the reader beware. You are not getting "all the news that's fit to print" about Israel. You are getting only the "news" that its reporters and editors fit into their preconceived and biased narrative.

I challenge the Columbia School of Journalism, or any other objective academic institution, to conduct a study of the *Times* "reporting" on the Israeli-Palestinian conflict over the last few years. The results will shame the *Times* and caution its readers to skeptically evaluate what passes as "reporting." (If the study went back to reporting on the Holocaust or the establishment of Israel, it would be even worse.)

In the meantime, the *Times* must publicly, clearly, and substantively apologize for its reporter lying about "powerful . . . rabbis" and explain how its editors could permit such an obviously anti-Semitic canard to be published on its pages. Quietly eliminating the offending words from its online version is cowardly and insufficient. It must acknowledge the harm that its false reporting has caused.

Anti-Zionism and anti-Semitism have become rampant and widely acceptable among some in academia. Recently a University of Chicago professor who has contributed to this bigotry attacked me.

I regard it is an honor to be attacked or mocked by anti-Semites or enablers of anti-Semitism. As a frequent target of such bigots, I generally ignore their garbage. But when the enablers are professors at a distinguished university, it is essential to expose them and respond.

The University of Chicago has two professors who fit into this sordid category. To understand why the shoe fits, we must go back to the publication a few years ago of an overtly anti-Semitic book, *The Wandering Who?*, by an admitted Jew-hater named Gilad Atzmon.

Atzmon, who was born in Israel, declared himself a "proud, self-hating Jew," with "contempt" for "the Jew in me." His writings both online and in his book brim with classic anti-Semitic motifs borrowed from Nazi publications.

Throughout his writings, Atzmon argues that Jews "do try to seek to control the world."

Here are a few of Atzmon's statements:

- Jews are "evil and a "menace to humanity."
- "With Fagin and Shylock in mind, Israeli barbarism and organ trafficking seem to be just other events in an endless hellish continuum."
- "The Homo Zionicus quickly became a mass murderer, detached from any recognized form of ethical thinking and engaged in a colossal crime against humanity."
- "If Iran and Israel fight a nuclear war that kills tens of millions of people, some may be bold enough to argue that Hitler might have been right after all."
- Children should question, "how the teacher could know that these accusations of Jews making Matza out of young Goyim's blood were indeed empty or groundless."
- "The Holocaust religion is probably as old as the Jews themselves."
- The history of Jewish persecution is a "myth," and if there was any persecution the Jews brought it on themselves.
- "Jews may have managed to drop their God, but they have maintained goy-hating and racist ideologies at the heart of their newly emerging secular political identity. This explains why some Talmudic goy-hating elements have been transformed within the Zionist discourse into genocidal practices."

Finally, Atzmon repeatedly declared that Israel is worse than the Nazis, and he actually has actually "apologized" to the Nazis for having earlier compared them to Israel:

> Too many of us including me tend to equate Israel to Nazi Germany. Rather often I myself join others and argue that Israelis are the Nazis of our time. I want to take this opportunity to amend my statement

Israelis are not the Nazis of our time and the Nazis were not the Israelis of their time. Israel, is in fact far worse than Nazi Germany.

In light of the manifestly unhinged bigotry, it should come as no surprise that even some of the most hardcore anti-Israel activists have shunned Atzmon out of fear that his naked anti-Semitism will discredit their cause. Tony Greenstein, a self-styled "anti-Zionist," denounced *The Wandering Who?* as "a poisonous anti-Semitic tome." Sue Blackwell, who co-wrote the Association of University Teachers' motion to boycott Israeli universities in 2005, removed all links to Atzmon from her website. Socialist Worker, a website that frequently refers to Israeli "apartheid" and publishes articles with titles such as "Israel's Murderous Violence," removed an interview with Atzmon and called the evidence of Atzmon's anti-Semitism "damning." At least ten authors associated with Atzmon's leftist publisher have called on it to distance itself from Atzmon's views, explaining that the "thrust of Atzmon's work is to normalize and legitimize anti-Semitism."

Hardcore neo-Nazis, racists, anti-Semites, and Holocaust deniers, on the other hand, have happily counted Atzmon as one of their own. David Duke, America's premier white supremacist, has posted more than a dozen of Atzmon's articles on his website, praising the author for "writ[ing] such fine articles exposing the evil of Zionism and Jewish supremacism." Israel Shamir, a Holocaust denier—who has said that "we must deny the concept of Holocaust without doubt and hesitation" and who has argued that Jews ritually murdered Christian children for their blood—refers to Atzmon as a "good friend" and called him one of "the shining stars of the battle" against "the Jewish alliance."

But neither Atzmon's well-established reputation for anti-Semitism nor the copious anti-Semitic filth that fills *The Wandering Who?* has deterred Professor John Mearsheimer and Brian Leitner of the University of Chicago from endorsing Atzmon's work.

Mearsheimer, the Harrison Distinguished Service Professor of Political Science at the University of Chicago and a member of the American Academy of Arts and Sciences, wrote a blurb for *The*

Wandering Who?, calling it a "fascinating" book that "should be read widely by Jews and non-Jews alike."

Brian Leiter, the Llewellyn Professor of Jurisprudence at the University of Chicago Law School, dismissed the reaction to the book and to Mearsheimer's endorsement as "hysterical" and not "advance[ing] honest intellectual discourse," though he acknowledges not having read Atzmon's book. On the basis of having perused one brief interview with Atzmon, Leiter was prepared to defend him against charges that he is an anti-Semite as well as a Holocaust denier, calling him a "cosmopolitan."

These professors are not merely defending Atzmon's *right* to publish such a book, they are endorsing its *contents* and denying that its author is an anti-Semite.

Mearsheimer has defended his endorsement against attacks by me and others by questioning whether his critics have even read Atzmon's book. Well, I have read every word of it, as well as many of Atzmon's blog posts. No one who has read this material could escape the conclusion that Atzmon freely admits: his writings cross the line from anti-Zionism to crass anti-Semitism.

Not content to defend Atzmon against charges that he is an anti-Semite or Holocaust denier, Leitner has made it his calling to attack and mock me. In his most recent screed, he suggests that I never "publish" anything besides "op-eds, blog posts, and Tweets." He deliberately ignores the 50 books I have published on subjects ranging across terrorism, criminal law, the Fifth Amendment, the Declaration of Dependence, Thomas Jefferson, human rights, freedom of speech, law and psychiatry, freedom of religion, the Bible, and the two subjects he most abhors—Israel and the Jewish future. He also ignores the dozens of law review articles published in the *Harvard Law Review*, the *Yale Law Journal*, and many others. One hallmark of the classic anti-Semite and enabler of anti-Semitism is to omit the positive contributions of Jews and to distort and mock their accomplishments.

When Mearsheimer and Leitner first manifested their bigotry, I challenged them to a debate. Neither accepted. I repeat my challenge now. It is easy to come down on the side of anti-Semitism, especially today on university campuses. One can only imagine the reaction if Chicago professors wrote in praise of David Duke, deny-ing he is anti-Black. Atzmon is every bit the bigot as Duke. The only difference is that Atzmon targets only Jews. And today that seems to make a difference. So, let us see if Mearsheimer and Leitner have the courage to defend their complicity with Jew-hatred.

Sometimes the source of anti-Semitism is a distinguished per-son who has done much good in other areas. Among people with such mixed records are Henry Ford, Charles Lindbergh, Roald Dahl, Ezra Pound, T. S. Eliot, Fyodor Dostoevsky, and Richard Wagner. The most recent example of a "good anti-Semite" is the late Bishop Desmond Tutu.

Tutu did much good in fighting apartheid but he also has a long history of ugly hatred toward the Jewish people, the Jewish religion, and the Jewish state. He not only believed in anti-Semitism, he actively promoted and legitimized Jew-hatred among his many fol-lowers and admirers around the world.

Tutu minimized the suffering of those killed in the Holocaust. He attacked the "Jewish"—not Israeli—"lobby" as too "powerful" and "scary." He invoked classic anti-Semitic stereotypes and tropes about Jewish "arrogance," "power," and "money." He characterized Jews as a "peculiar people," and has accused "the Jews" of causing many of the world's problems.

Tutu's good deeds should not shield him from accountability for his long history of anti-Jewish bigotry.

Let the record speak for itself, so that history may judge Tutu on the basis of his own words—words that he often repeated and that others repeat, because Tutu was a role model for so many people around the world. Here are some of Tutu's hateful words, carefully documented in a petition by prominent South Africans to terminate him as a "patron" of the two South African Holocaust Centers, because he used his sta-tus with these fine institutions as legitimization for his anti-Jewish rhetoric. I have publicized Tutu's evil words in the past, but they war-rant republication now that he is being lionized all over the world.

He minimized the suffering of those murdered in the Holocaust by asserting that "the gas chambers" made for "a neater death" than did apartheid. He complained of "the Jewish Monopoly of the Holocaust," and demanded that Jews "forgive" the Nazis, while himself refusing to forgive the "Jewish people" for "perse-cute[ing] others."

Tutu asserted that Zionism has "very many parallels with racism," thus echoing the notorious and discredited "Zionism equals racism" resolution passed by the General Assembly of the United Nations and subsequently rescinded. He accused the Jews of Israel of doing "things that even Apartheid South Africa had not done." He said that "the Jews thought they had a monopoly of God: Jesus was angry that they could shut out other human beings." He implied that Israel might someday consider it an option "to perpetrate genocide and exterminate all Palestinians."

He complained that Americans "are scared . . . to say wrong is wrong because the Jewish lobby is powerful—very powerful." He accused Jews—not Israelis—of exhibiting "an arrogance—the arro-gance of power because Jews are a powerful lobby in this land and all kinds of people woo their support."

"You know as as well as I do that, somehow, the Israeli gov-ernment is placed on a pedestal [in the US] and to criticize it is to be immediately dubbed anti-Semitic, as if Palestinians were not Semitic."

He compared Israel to Hitler's Germany, Stalin's Soviet Union and apartheid South Africa, saying that they too were once "very powerful" but they "bit the dust," as will "unjust" Israel.

He denied that Israel is a "civilized democracy" and singled out Israel—one of the world's most open democracies—as a nation guilty of "censorship of their media." He urged the Cape Town Opera to refuse to perform George Gershwin's *Porgy and Bess* in Tel Aviv and called for a total cultural boycott of Jewish Israel, while encouraging performers to visit the most repressive regimes in the world.

* * *

Sometimes the attack on Jews can be subtle and come from mis-guided friends. Recently one such friend called for a change in the

First Amendment that would endanger the status of American Jews as first-class citizens.

General Michael Flynn in his speech to the "ReAwaken America" Tour said:

> If we are going to have one nation under God, which we must, we have to have one religion. One nation under God and one religion under God.

The Framers of our Constitution—particularly Madison, Jefferson, and Hamilton—would be turning over in their graves to hear a retired general and former national security adviser trying to undercut the First Amendment, which unequivocally declares that "Congress shall make no law respecting an establishment of religion, or prohibiting the free exercise thereof." Flynn would establish one religion—presumably his!

This is not the first time that religious zealots have tried to Christianize America. When the Constitution was ratified, critics called it "the Godless constitution." The Declaration of Independence had invoked God, because it had to: there was no legal basis for revolting against Britain—only a moral or religious basis. But the Constitution was drafted to protect the rights of all Americans, even non-Christians and those who were deists, agnostic, or atheists. During the Civil War, some Christian ministers predicted that the Union would lose unless they added Jesus to the constitution. All these efforts to Christianize our constitution have failed.

The Constitution mentions religion only three times: 1) to preclude the establishment of religion; 2) to preclude any prohibition on the free exercise of religion: and 3) to preclude any religious test for holding office under the United States. At the time of the framing, nearly all Americans were protestant Christians, but there was great conflict among protestant sects. The Constitution forbid the Congress to pick and choose among these sects to establish one religion.

General Flynn was raised as a Roman Catholic. At the time of the constitution, Catholics were discriminated against in a number of states, including Massachusetts. The First Amendment was designed to protest Catholics and Jews from becoming second-class citizens.

As President George Washington wrote to the Hebrew congregation in Newport Rhode Island in 1770:

> The Citizens of the United States of America have a right to applaud themselves for having given to mankind examples of an enlarged and liberal policy: A policy worthy of imitation. All possess alike liberty of conscience and immunities of citizenship. It is not no more that toleration is spoken of, as if it was by the indulgence of one class of people, that another enjoyed the exercise of their inherent natural rights. For happily the Government of the United States, which gives to bigotry no sanction, to persecution no assistance requires only that they who live under its protection should demean themselves as good citizens, in giving it on all occasions their effectual support.

Some supporters of Flynn have claimed that the one religion he espouses is a broad and incisive one: "Judeo-Christianity," but not broad enough to include Islam, Buddhism, or the dozens of other faiths that have long been part of the American mosaic. Other religious fundamentalists will surely insist that their own brand of Christianity—say Evangelical Baptists—should be selected as the official national religion. Still others will say that each state should be able to establish its own official religion. None of these violations of the First Amendment would work as a matter of policy, even if the Constitution permitted it.

Consider Israel which is the nation state of the Jewish people. Under its basic laws, Muslims and Christians have equal rights, but plainly the Jewish religion has far greater influence in practice. But even in a so called "Jewish state," there is conflict among branches of Judaism: Charedi, modern Orthodox, conservative, reform, and reconstructionist.

In the United States it would be far worse because of the enormous religious and cultural diversity within our population. It would be bad not only for civil liberties but also for religion, which would become too dependent on the government.

Most Republicans with whom I have spoken about the Flynn idea have rejected it categorically. They include even rabid Trump supporters and religious fundamentalists. It's a bad and dangerous idea and should quickly be relegated to the wastebin of history. General Flynn, who is not an anti-Semite, should withdraw his proposal that would further divide an already divided nation. The last thing we need is a religious war, in which different sects vie with each other for dominance.

The Framers were wise enough to devise the first constitutional structure in history that separated church and state. To create a national religion would undo that wise separation.

The United States is the envy of the world when it comes to religious freedom. Religious conflict—even warfare—is rampant in the Mideast and other regions. We should count our blessings for our Constitution. It ain't broke, so don't break it.

What is broke and needs fixing is the unprincipled double standard bigotry that so many on the hard left, in academia and in the media display toward the only nation state of the Jewish people.

CHAPTER 8

Unprincipled and Partisan Approaches to Voting Rights

—————

The right of all eligible voters to cast their votes in elections should be a principled goal of all good people and both major political parties. Voter fraud and ballots cast by ineligible voters should be prevented. An appropriate balance must be struck between these two policies, but the problem of disqualifying and discouraging eligible voters is far more serious than the problem of voter fraud. Yet the fear of the latter is often used as an excuse for the former.

There is nothing wrong with requiring some valid form of identification to vote, as long as obtaining such IDs is easy and does not discriminate against certain voters. Many on the left who favor vaccine IDs oppose voter IDs, and vice versa. Voting eligibility, like everything else in politics, has become a partisan issue with Democrats favoring the side of the balance that supports expanded eligibility, and Republicans favoring fraud prevention. Both sides claim they are acting on principle, and that may be true. But it is also true that the demography of expanded voting favors Democrats, and the demography of preventing voter fraud favors Republicans. Would each side be making the same principled arguments if the shoe were on the other foot—if expanded voting favored the Republicans?

A good test case of the conflict between principle and partisanship is the movement for District of Columbia statehood.

As a liberal Democrat, I favor the right of residents of the city of Washington D.C. to elect senators and voting members of Congress. (They already vote for presidential electors under the 23rd Amendment.) But I do not necessarily support statehood for the District of Columbia. My position is neither inconsistent nor paradoxical. The right to vote is individual and personal. The right to statehood is political and collective. Supporting the former does not necessarily entail supporting the latter.

The Constitution provides for the existence of a "district" to be "the seat of the government of the United States" in an area not exceeding 10 square miles that is created "by cessation of particular states." That district is not to be a state. There is no constitutional minimum for the size of the seat of government. Nor does the Constitution preclude Congress from ceding some of the land back to the states that originally ceded it to form the district.

These constitutional parameters provide congress with three realistic options: 1) to maintain the status quo that denies residents of the district the right to vote for senators and voting members of congress; 2) to create a new state comprised of nearly all the residential areas of the city, while preserving the status of the small governmental areas as the non-state seat of government; or 3) not to create a new state but to cede the residential areas back to Maryland, while preserving the governmental areas as the non-state capital.

Most Democrats and residents of the District of Columbia favor the second alternative—statehood with two senators and one voting member of Congress. Most Republicans favor the first alternative—preserving the status quo. I favor the third—ceding the residential areas back to Maryland, so that the residents of the city of Washington get to vote for Maryland senators and members of congress, without creating a new state.

Advocates of statehood base their claim primarily on the right of Washington residents to vote. Opponents argue that statehood would assure the Democrats two additional senators and one additional voting member of Congress and that the push for statehood, as distinguished from voting rights, is motivated largely by partisan considerations. They point to the last new states—Alaska and

Hawaii—that were admitted in tandem without partisan advantage to either side, because one was Republican and the other Democrat. They point out that if a Democratic Congress could create a new Democratic state, a Republican Congress could retaliate by dividing Idaho into two states, North and South Idaho, and Wyoming into East and West Wyoming, thus assuring additional Republican votes in the Senate and House. The Constitution permits Congress to create a new state out of an existing one, with the consent of the state legislature, as was done with Maine and West Virginia.

Some argue that granting statehood to DC would not only shift the balance <u>between</u> the parties in favor of the Democrats, but it might also shift the balance <u>within</u> the Democratic party in favor of the "progressive" wing of the party. (I put progressive in quotes, because that wing is anything but progressive on freedom of speech, due process, and other constitutional rights.) They point out that Democratic voters in Washington tend to be more to the left—as city voters tend to be—than Democrats are in general. (Statehood would create the only all city-state.) Whether or not that is true today, and will remain true in the future, it is clear that DC statehood would favor the Democrats both in the short and long term.

If the principled goal of changing the status of the District of Columbia is to fully enfranchise its residents, that admirable goal can be accomplished by adopting the third alternative—ceding the residential areas back to Maryland.

At this time of hyper-partisan divisions, when the criteria for political action seems to be more about partisan advantage than the principled good of the nation as a whole, the last thing we need is yet another divisive partisan battle that turns on which party is currently in control.

The residents of the city of Washington should receive full voting rights without shifting the political balance. That desirable end can be achieved only by making its residential areas part of Maryland and maintaining the largely non-residential areas between the White House and the Supreme Court as the non-state seat of government.

The shifting of the political balance of power to the left <u>within</u> the Democratic Party may also result in a shift of power <u>between</u> Democrats and Republicans, to the advantage of the latter.

Every day I get several blast emails from Democratic fundraisers warning that the Democrats may lose upcoming elections unless they can raise substantial amounts of money. On a recent morning alone, I received solicitations from Nancy Pelosi, Stacey Abrams, and Alexandria Ocasio-Cortez demanding a contribution because—in Pelosi's words—"my House majority is in severe danger."

But money is not the reason why Democrats may lose in 2022 and 2024. The reason has far more to do with ideology.

American voters tend to be centrist, or at least far more moderate than the Democratic Party's left-leaning activists. That is why Joe Biden won the 2020 primaries and general election, and why the Democrats now control—albeit narrowly—the Senate and the House. Moderates made the difference in swing states and districts.

Recently, however, the Democratic leadership has given far too much power and influence to the small number of loud radical extremists in the party. It is as if AOC is the majority leader of the House and Ilhan Omar her deputy. The Squad managed to derail an initial proposal to fund Israel's Iron Dome. Fortunately, this effort was rebuffed by a subsequent overwhelming vote of support. But then Andy Levin, not a member of the Squad but a left-leaning Democrat, introduced legislation that would falsely declare the Gaza Strip, the Western Wall, and the Jewish Quarter of Jerusalem to be "occupied territory." His benighted bill had the support of several mainstream Democrats. Although the defunding of Iron Dome was voted against by the vast majority of Democrats and the Levin bill would probably suffer the same fate, many pro-Israel moderates are concerned that such anti-Israel legislation is even being proposed.

It is not only with regard to the Israeli-Palestinian conflict that the left wing of the Democratic Party is flexing its muscles. There is a discernible trend leftward within the party and an unwillingness to condemn the extremists. Many centrist voters now see the Democrats as the party of left-wing radicals, who are intolerant of dissent, impatient with due process, and critical of the free-market economy.

As one influential pollster warned: The Democratic Party is "trapped in an echo chamber of Twitter activists and woke staff members," and most Democratic voters are not woke.

Moderate Democrats may be overstating the shift to the left within the Democratic Party as a whole, but they are right about the perception and also about the trends. They are right because the leaders of the Democratic Party refuse to condemn the radicals on its hard-left fringe.

They remain silent in the face of bigotry for fear that public criticism may lose them votes among the increasing number of young people who sympathize with the "Ben & Jerry" radical wing of the party. They also fear pushback from old radicals—now rich contributors in Hollywood, on Wall Street, and in Silicon Valley—who belong to the Larry David and Michael Moore knee-jerk fringe.

If centrist Democrats are asked to cast their lot with police defunders, critical race theory propagandists, radical teachers' unions, BDS advocates, identity politicians, anti-free market socialists and the like, many will stay home or vote Republican.

The Democratic Party cannot win as the party of the extreme left. Nor can it long endure trying to be all things to all people. Its leadership must decide whether their tent includes intolerant bigots of the hard left—just as Republicans must decide whether their tent includes intolerant bigots of the hard right. If the Democratic establishment insists on currying favor with these extremists, its leaders must at the very least criticize their bigotry and not reward them as Pelosi did by putting Ilhan Omar—an anti-Semitic bigot—on the Foreign Relations Committee, and posing smilingly with that anti-Semite on the cover of *Rolling Stone*!

For the Democrats to win—and I hope they do—they must denounce and marginalize their extremists, even if that means losing a few votes. The Democratic tent is large, reflecting a wide diversity of views, but it is not large enough to include anti-Jewish, anti-American, anti-free speech, and anti-free market extremists.

If they continue down the current dangerous path, the Democrats will become a minority party, as the British Labor Party became under the radical and bigoted leadership of Jeremy Corbyn, who was supported by Bernie Sanders and would fit perfectly in the Squad.

Both parties would benefit from a bit more principled bipartisanship. And so would the nation as a whole.

CHAPTER 9

The Partisan Divide over Vaccine Mandates

———

The threat of COVID and the variants, and the responses to it—especially vaccine and masking mandates—have divided the nation and the world. The division is not strictly along party lines. Some on the fringe left are anti-vaxxers. But Republicans tend to be more suspicious of government mandates, especially when they are imposed by Democrats and Democratic officials such as President Joe Biden.

President Biden has issued a series of executive orders—without express legislative authority—mandating vaccination or weekly testing for a significant percentage of American workers. Since the announcement, I have been besieged with calls, emails, and media requests all asking the same question: is it constitutional? I've just completed writing a book on precisely that subject, entitled *The Case for Vaccine Mandates*, in which I analyze the legal issues surrounding vaccination, masking, and related mandates.

Here is my conclusion: it depends!

It depends on the following three questions, all raised by Biden's actions:

1. Does the federal—as distinguished from state—government have jurisdiction over COVID and vaccine mandates?

2. If the federal government has (or shares) such jurisdiction, may it constitutionally require, even with exceptions, workers to be vaccinated against their will or as a condition of their employment?
3. If the federal government has the constitutional power to mandate such vaccinations, can that order be made by the executive, as distinguished from the legislative branch of the federal government?

Unless all three questions are answered in the affirmative, I predicted that President Biden's orders would not pass the test of legality.

The first question is easy. Yes, the federal government has jurisdiction over America's response to a pandemic that does not recognize state boundaries. So do the states, but the supremacy clause of the Constitution has been interpreted to mean that where there is joint jurisdiction, and a conflict between federal and state law arises, federal law prevails.

The second question is harder, but courts would likely sustain a properly enacted law, with appropriate exceptions, that mandated vaccination as a last resort. There is a Supreme Court decision on compelled vaccinations, but it is a 1905 state case that carried a small fine for noncompliance. Subsequent lower court decisions point in the same direction. So it is likely, but far from certain with this high court, that a properly enacted statute mandating vaccination, with exceptions, or conditioning employment and other benefits on vaccination or testing would be upheld.

That brings us to the third question: can such a sweeping "emergency" mandate, that is not limited in time, be authorized by the president without explicit legislation by Congress? That is the most challenging question of all. It is daunting because the constitutional authority of the presidency has been expanding since the New Deal and its limits are constantly being tested by presidents of both parties. This is evidenced by the wars we have fought in recent decades without a congressional declaration of war, and more recently by Donald Trump's border wall and Biden's vaccine mandate.

Presidents generally cite broad and vague congressional authority for their actions. Sometimes the courts accept this authority, and sometimes they don't.

One point is clear: both sides are exaggerating their constitutional and statutory claims. Some proponents of the Biden mandate assure us that its constitutionality "is completely clear," while some opponents are certain that it is "utterly lawless." I predicted that the question could go either way. In such a close case, President Biden is justified in doing what he believes to be in the public interest and leaving it to courts to decide. That is what FDR did in the 1930s. The situation would be different if it were clear that Biden's actions were unconstitutional, and he knew it: the president has sworn to uphold the Constitution and may not act in a clearly unconstitutional manner and leave it to the courts. But that is not the case here; these are close questions, and it is not surprising that a closely divided court ruled that the president did not have the authority under OSHA to mandate vaccines for the roughly 100 million people who work for large private companies. That decision was 6–3, with Chief Justice John Roberts and Justice Brett Kavanaugh voting with the majority and against the three "liberal" justices. These two justices then joined the three liberals in upholding the mandate for health workers. These were not final decisions—the issues involved stays of lower court judgments. But as a matter of constitutional law and statutory interpretation, the Supreme Court's two decisions are probably correct.

Although these decisions may appear inconsistent on a superficial level, they make sense when looked at from a purely legal perspective. In my recent book, *The Case for Vaccine Mandates*, I predicted this outcome. One section of my book is entitled "In a Democracy Who Decides?" That was precisely the question posed by Justice Neil Gorsuch in his concurring opinion for the OSHA case.

Under our federal system of separation of powers, Congress gets to make laws that are within the authority of the federal government. The executive enforces these laws, and the judiciary decides whether they are constitutional.

The judiciary also decides whether Congress authorized the executive branch to make certain decisions. In this case, a majority decided that the OSHA law enacted by Congress did not grant authority to the executive branch for so broad a mandate. But a 5–4 majority then decided that Congress did authorize administrative agencies to condition receipt of federal health benefits on vaccine mandates.

As I wrote in my book, it is far better for Congress, rather than the executive, to make broad-based, controversial decisions that affect so many millions of Americans. Administrative agencies are far less representative of the will of the people than is the elected Congress.

So, the split decision was probably correct as a matter of law, though confusing to many as a matter of policy. Few Americans will be satisfied with it. Those who favor mandates will be frustrated by the Supreme Court's OSHA decision, while those who oppose mandates will disagree with the decision regarding health care workers. It is not the job of the Supreme Court to satisfy Americans. Its job is to be faithful to the objective rule of law. There are good arguments on all sides of these issues and a divided decision by a divided Court should surprise no one.

Many issues still remain open as a result of these two decisions. One involves the power of states to enact laws mandating vaccination, or to enact laws prohibiting vaccine mandates. It is possible to imagine directly conflicting outcomes: New York and California might enact legislation requiring vaccine mandates for large private employers, while Texas and Georgia might pass laws prohibiting employers from requiring vaccination. Although COVID does not respect state boundaries, the Constitution may well permit different rules for different states, especially if Congress does not act to federalize the issue of vaccine mandates.

So stay tuned. This is not the last you will hear from the Supreme Court regarding vaccine mandates. The most fundamental issue is whether a properly enacted federal law mandating vaccinations, with appropriate exceptions and based on current science, would be upheld by the current Supreme Court. This may never come to pass, because it is unlikely that Congress would enact so broad a mandate. But if it did, the five justices who upheld the health provider mandate might well uphold a more general mandate. But that is far from certain in light of the careful language the justices used in this case.

It's far from over. All Americans should hope that whatever decisions are rendered, they will be based on constitutional principles, not partisan preferences.

Chapter 10

As a Matter of Principle, Are We a Systematically Racist Nation?

———

Since the beginning of our history as a nation—and even before—race has been a divisive factor. Our "compromise Constitution" compromised even on the issue of whether people of color count as full human beings for political purposes. We fought a civil war primarily about race. And we segregated our citizens based on race. We were surely a systemic racist nation back then. Racism persists and permeates various aspects of American life. But is it fair to characterize the current United States as a systemically racist nation?

The welcome adoption of Juneteenth as a national holiday celebrating the end of slavery confirms what should have been obvious for at least a generation—namely, that we are no longer a systemically racist nation. To the contrary, as a matter of principle if not always practice, we have become a systemically <u>anti</u>-racist nation, albeit with far too many pockets of residual racism, particularly in certain areas of life. But our essential systems—our laws, politics, media, education, religion, corporations—have all become discernibly anti-racist, in every meaningful sense of that term.

By "systemically" racist and anti-racist I mean to describe how these important instruments of governance impact on the role of race in America today. A comparison with the not so distant past will make my point.

When I was born in 1938, the United States was systemically racist, sexist, homophobic, anti-Catholic, anti-Asian, anti-Hispanic, and anti-Semitic. The bigotry came from the top down. It was an accepted part of the greater American system of governance. It was enforced, or at least tolerated, legally. It was systematic in the sense that it was pervasive, acknowledged, and accepted by our political and legal structure.

Discrimination, approved by the majority of Americans and tolerated by law, determined who could run for president, be admitted to or become the head of elite universities, immigrate, live in certain neighborhoods, be hired by many corporations and the largest law firms, be accepted in various social and athletic clubs, play major professional sports, be appointed a Supreme Court justice. There was systematic, pervasive, and legally permitted discrimination in favor of white, Protestant, heterosexual men. All others were, at best, second-class citizens, with some being third- and fourth-class.

Many of the most important benefits of our political, economic, and social systems were withheld, in whole or in part, from individuals based on race, religion, ethnicity, gender, sexual orientation, and other invidious factors. The discrimination against African Americans was the most systemic, since it was part of our constitutional history. But the discrimination against other groups was systemic as well.

In 1922, Harvard's most prominent Jewish professor, Harry A. Wolfson, proclaimed that being born Jewish was comparable to being born "blind," "deaf," or "lame." It meant being deprived of "many social goods and advantages," he said. He urged his Jewish students to "submit to fate," as if they had been born hunchbacked. He also urged them *not* to "foolishly struggle against it" because "there are certain problems of life for which no solution is possible." What Wolfson was telling his students was that anti-Semitism was systemic, unchallengeable, and permanent. I can imagine an African American leader in 1922, and even later, telling his students the same thing. Both were descriptively correct back then.

In the 1920s, '30s and even '50s, we still had Jim Crow laws, racist immigration restrictions, and rules that permitted—sometimes required[1]—discrimination of all sorts. A liberal president, Franklin D. Roosevelt, ordered the detention of thousands of American citizens based exclusively on their race and national origin. We were a systemically bigoted nation, and our Constitution, born of compromise with slavery (which Martin Luther King aptly characterized as a "birth defect"), accepted this bigotry. Even after the enactment of the 13th, 14th, and 15th Amendments to the Constitution, the courts refused to implement the demand for equal protection of the law until the second half of the 20th century—and then only with "deliberate speed," which was more deliberate than speedy.

The second half of the past century, following World War II, saw major changes in law, practice, and attitudes.

We have seen the end of lawful segregation as well as the election of Catholic and Black presidents and vice presidents. For generations, the Supreme Court was comprised entirely of white Protestant males. Then a handful of Catholics were appointed, and a "Jewish seat" was established, but it remained a dominantly white Protestant male institution. Now the high court has only one white Protestant male. The other justices are Catholics and Jews, three of whom are women (a fourth—the first Black woman—has been confirmed). Jews, women, and Blacks have become presidents of many major universities. Neighborhoods can no longer be "restricted"—at least as a matter of law. Corporations, law firms, businesses and most private clubs are not allowed to discriminate. All sports leagues are integrated. Many groups that were previously discriminated against have members in Congress, in state legislatures, and in other elected or appointed offices. Most universities and many other institutions have race-based affirmative action programs.

We have a long way to go in eliminating the residues of bigotry from our institutions—some, such as law enforcement, more than others. But compared to 1960, it is difficult to conclude that

---

1   My late father-in-law, a respected pharmacist in South Carolina, was precluded by law from eating lunch with his friend, an African American doctor, at the pharmacy lunch counter.

the racism that remains in this country—and it is still considerable, especially in some areas—can be fairly categorized as "systemic."

To the contrary, what has *become* systemic over the past six decades, and especially in recent years, is anti-racism. The laws have changed. Policies have changed. Practices and attitudes have changed, though not enough. We are a very different country systemically. Racism no longer has the imprimatur of law, politics, religion, or the media. It comes primarily from the bottom up, rather than the top down. In 1960 and before, candidates and other leaders would proudly proclaim their racist beliefs. Today, those who still harbor such beliefs—and there are still too many of them—need to hide them precisely because racism is no longer systemically accepted, as it was as recently as 60 years ago.

So, no, we are not the systemically and top-down racist country we once were. We have become a systemically top-down anti-racist country with far too much bottom-up racism that we must end, especially in some important areas like law enforcement. But let's not deny the real progress we have made as we celebrate our newest national holiday.

The underlined principle of equality, differently defined for different people or groups, is largely prevailing over the practice of prejudice, but we still have a long way to go if we are to make real Martin Luther King's dream of being judged not by the color of one's skin, but by the content of one's character.

The current question that divides Americans is whether MLK's dream can become reality if race remains a factor—in this case an affirmative factor—in university admission decisions, qualifications for Supreme Court and other governmental and private positions.

The Supreme Court's decision to grant review of the race-based affirmative action programs of Harvard and the University of North Carolina may answer that question if it rules that race alone will not be permitted as a criterion for college admissions.

It requires only four votes for *certiorari* to be granted, so there is a possibility that a majority may still favor the status quo. But it is more likely that at least five justices are seeking to reconsider the role of race in admissions, as well as other decisions.

Because Harvard is a private university and UNC is public, the court may have selected these two cases together for review to distinguish between the private and the public. But this is too unlikely, especially in light of the high court's 5–4 decision upholding a vaccine mandate for private hospitals that receive federal funding. The line between public and private has become blurred as a matter of law.

There are three clear votes on the court for upholding race as a possible criterion (Justices Stephen Breyer, Sonia Sotomayor, and Elena Kagan) and three votes against it (Justices Clarence Thomas, Samuel Alito, and Neil Gorsuch). Chief Justice John Roberts may side with the liberals even if he disagrees that race is a constitutionally permissible factor, because he places considerable emphasis on precedent. Justices Brett Kavanaugh and Amy Coney Barret both had university teaching backgrounds and have lived with race-based admissions policies all of their professional lives; it is difficult to predict which way this experience will cut.

It is also difficult to predict whether any of the three uncertain justices might agree with retired Justice Sandra Day O'Connor's argument, now withdrawn, that race-based affirmative action should have a statute of limitations—say 25 years, which has long expired since she first suggested it.

Finally, there has never been a time in recent history when race has ostensibly mattered more—in education, in health care, in policing, in voting rights, in entertainment, in business, and in other aspects of American life. For the justices to rule that race shouldn't matter at all in college admissions policies would be to confront a powerful current reality.

As an abstract constitutional matter, the issue seems clear: The son of a Black hedge fund billionaire who went to Exeter should not be given admissions advantage over a poor white woman with no political connections.

But the issue is rarely presented to college admissions committees or to courts in so abstract a manner. Race often, though not always, serves as a surrogate for factors that are considered in admissions decisions, including poverty, opportunity, and overcoming handicaps. Admissions committees can continue to consider all of these and other issues even if race alone is rejected, though their job might be harder without the far simpler shortcut of using race.

There is another issue that the courts have not adequately confronted: the presence of a significant number of minorities on entering a college class. If there is an educational advantage to having a number of people of a particular race in the entering class, can that number be turned into a floor? And if there is a floor for some, does that necessarily mean there is a ceiling for others? In other words, are quotas inherent in any system of race-based affirmative action?

Nonetheless, even if the Supreme Court were to rule unequivocally that race alone can never be considered in admissions decisions by public universities or private ones that accept government funding, university admissions committees will figure out ways to factor in race without doing so overtly.

There undoubtedly will be more lawsuits challenging individual admissions decisions; the Supreme Court will not settle all the divisive issues surrounding race. It may, however, articulate an important principle that race alone can neither confer governmentally approved advantages or disadvantages.

It is ironic that while the justices are deliberating whether race can be considered in university admissions, the president announced that he will focus on race and gender in nominating the next justice. He did so and nominated an extremely well qualified Black woman—Judge Ketanji Brown Jackson, who has been confirmed by a largely party-line vote.

Imagine a president announcing that since no Muslim has ever been appointed to the Supreme Court, he pledges to nominate the first Muslim justice. That would undoubtedly be unconstitutional since Article VI of the Constitution specifies that "no religious Test shall ever be required as a Qualification to any Office or public Trust under the United States." The spirit of that prohibition—coupled with the 14th and 19th amendments—would certainly seem to apply to race and gender as well. It is wrong, and perhaps unconstitutional, for a president to impose a racial or gender test for nomination to the

Supreme Court. If a president were to announce that he intended to nominate only a white male, constitutional scholars would rightfully object. So, what is the difference?

Supporters of President Biden's announcement will argue that there is a big difference between <u>prohibiting</u> a person from serving based on religion, race, or gender, and affirmatively giving <u>preference</u> based on these criteria. That is sophistry. By limiting his choice to a Black woman, President Biden disqualified every non-Black woman and man in America. There are a considerable number of highly qualified Black women, and I would have applauded the nomination of any one of them as I did Judge Jackson. But that is not the issue. The issue is overt exclusion.

The Supreme Court has a long history of exclusion. For more than a century-and-a-quarter after the religious prohibition was incorporated into the Constitution, presidents excluded all Jewish candidates and most Catholic candidates. The Supreme Court was an institution reserved primarily for white Protestant males. That was wrong and unconstitutional. But two wrongs, even if one of them is a "good" wrong, do not make a constitutional right.

Judge Jackson, who was nominated and confirmed for the job, may suffer reputationally from the president's announcement. She is extremely well qualified. But she may well be regarded not as the most qualified <u>person</u>, but only as the most qualified <u>Black</u> <u>woman</u>. That is insulting, even if not intended to be. Senator Charles Schumer compounded President Biden's error by announcing that regardless of who the president nominated, she will be confirmed by the Democratic controlled Senate. That, too, politicizes the Supreme Court's nominating process. The Senate is supposed to deliberate on the qualifications of each nominee and confirm or reject her or him on the merits, not on the basis of who nominated her.

The Republicans engaged in partisan weaponization of the process when it refused to give a hearing to Judge Garland and then rushed through the confirmation of Judge Barrett. But again, two partisan wrongs do not make a constitutional right.

President Biden should have directed Attorney General Garland to prepare a list of the 25 most qualified nominees. No one should be excluded on the basis of race or gender. Such a list, if fairly compiled would include Black women. The president should then have selected his nominee from that list. If he had done so, he would be following the example of President Herbert Hoover, who asked his Attorney General to prepare a list of nominees to replace the great Justice Oliver Wendell Holmes Jr.

Historians recount that Hoover showed the list to Republican Senator William Borah. Benjamin Cardozo's name was at the bottom, along with the three reasons he should not be nominated, despite his great distinction.

"Cardoza [sic]—Jew, Democrat, New York" Borah glanced at it, and, believing Cardozo should be at the top, told Hoover, "Your list is alright, but you handed it to me upside down . . . Cardozo belongs as much to Idaho as to New York." As for Cardozo's being a Jew, Borah reportedly told Hoover, "Anyone who raises the question of race is unfit to advise you concerning so important a matter."

Cardozo was nominated and confirmed.

We live in an age of identity politics, when race and gender seem to count more than merit. The Supreme Court may soon confront that issue when it decides whether Harvard and the University of North Carolina violated the law by apparently preferring African American over Asian American applicants. If the justices decide that race alone may not properly be considered as a factor in admissions, they may well send a message to President Biden and future presidents regarding race and gender as a criteria for nominations to the high court.

Race, gender, and ideology sometimes are conflated, especially with regard to judicial appointments. This seems to be the case with President Biden's nomination of more than 20 former public defenders, many of whom were Black women.

Some of the same Republicans who praised me, a Democrat, for defending former President Trump against impeachment are now attacking Biden's judicial nominees for the clients they represented as public defenders.

Judge Jackson worked in the D.C. public defender's office early in her career and was assigned to represent defendants accused of terrorism and other heinous crimes. She did her job well. But now some

Republicans are accusing her and other former public defenders of doing their jobs too well.

Arianna Freeman, a nominee for a Court of Appeals seat, was asked if she regretted "trying to prevent" the execution of a defendant who was accused of a heinous double murder. Nina Morrison, another Biden nominee, was criticized for having "devoted your entire professional career to representing murderers, representing rapists, representing child molesters." And the Republican National Committee, in criticizing Judge Jackson, pointed to her "advocacy for these terrorists."

Democratic supporters of these nominees responded by invoking the "fundamental principle of the American justice system:" namely that "everyone has the constitutional right to be represented by counsel."

But some of these same Democrats attacked me and other lawyers for representing President Trump and other politically incorrect defendants. Now that the "shoe is on the other foot," these partisans have suddenly rediscovered a "fundamental principle" that they ignored just a few years ago. At that same time, Republican partisans have forgotten the principles they invoked in supporting my right and that of other lawyers to defend President Trump and other Republicans.

Senator Tom Cotton, a graduate of Harvard Law School, denied that criminal defense work was disqualifying but said that it was only appropriate to judge nominees by the cases they had accepted.

Well, I accepted the case of Donald Trump, and Senator Cotton praised me for it. John Adams accepted the case of the British soldiers accused of the Boston massacre. Abraham Lincoln, Daniel Webster, Clarence Darrow, Thurgood Marshall, Edward Bennett Williams and other distinguished defense attorneys would be disqualified from judicial service based on Senator Cotton's criteria.

And distinguished lawyers who defended prominent Republican politicians and causes might well be disqualified under the criteria applied by some Democrats to the representation of Donald Trump and by me and others.

Both sides may point out that there is a difference between defending accused <u>criminals</u> from prosecution, and defending an impeached <u>president</u> against removal, but each side will argue that one type of representation is <u>more</u> ethical than the other. Both would be wrong, self-serving, and hypocritical. It's too bad that Judge Jackson and some of her democratic supporters have gone out of their way to make excuses for who she defended. She was "assigned" to represent Guantanamo detainees. She didn't volunteer to defend them. Nor did she volunteer to represent the detainee she helped defend in private practice: she was asked to by a partner because she had previously worked on that detainee's case as a public defender. Finally, she was only doing her client's bidding when she helped write an amicus brief on behalf of organizations that supported the rights of detainees.

Her studied effort to distance herself from people she represented plays into the hands of those—both republicans and democrats—who seek to smear lawyers who voluntarily defend hated clients. These hypocrites sing the praises of John Adams volunteering to defend the British soldiers two and half centuries ago, but then condemn lawyers who volunteer today to defend politically incorrect clients. It's okay if they were "assigned," or if they did the bidding of their organizational clients.

But how would the senators have reacted if Jackson had said that she willingly and proudly volunteered to help set these accused criminals free? We will never know because Jackson didn't say that! Well, I'm saying it: I willingly and proudly defend accused murderers and terrorists. I am not "assigned" to do so. I choose to do it. And I wish Jackson had said the same thing, which I'm sure is true. The fact that she was advised by her handlers to make it sound like she was simply following orders tells us a great deal about the public acceptability— or lack thereof—of the constitutional role of defense counsel, and about the hypocrisy that both sides have about representing unpopular clients.

It is no surprise that hypocrisy is rampant in partisan politics. It is surprising that such hypocrisy is so transparent and obvious. The only "fundamental principle" to which both sides seem to agree is that there is a right to a zealous defense for <u>me</u> and <u>my</u> party but not for <u>you</u> and <u>your</u> party.

But just because the Democrats have been hypocritical about the fundamental nature of the right to counsel for "everyone" doesn't mean they are wrong now. No judicial candidate should be judged by the clients they have chosen or been assigned to represent. Judge Jackson and the other Biden nominees who have been defense attorneys should be judged by the quality of their work and other relevant factors. President Biden, who was himself a public defender for a brief time early in his career, should be praised for broadening the criteria for judicial nomination beyond the usual former prosecutors, corporate lawyers, and elite academics. Former public defenders will diversify the bench in an important way. Biden has, to his credit, nominated more than 20 former public defenders, each of whom should be judged on their individual merit.

As usual, some Democrats are trying to turn this into an issue of identity politics. Senator Richard Durbin has accused Republicans of opposing these nominees because they are "assertive women of color" who are soft on crime. But this is not about race or gender. It is about the right to a defense. History has shown that former defense attorneys can be very tough on crime when they become judges. Legendary defense lawyer Samuel Leibowitz, who vigorously defended notorious defendants including "The Scottsboro Boys," became the toughest law and order judge when he put on the robe. And Felix Frankfurter, who as a professor defended Sacco and Vanzetti, became a conservative justice.

The role of a judge is neither to be soft or hard on crime, but to be fair and to apply the law to the facts. To be sure, judges bring to the bench their experiences, backgrounds, ideologies, and attitudes with regard to crime and other hot button issues. That is precisely why presidents should nominate highly qualified judges whose qualifications include a wide variety of experiences in representing a diverse array of clients.

Judge—soon-to-be Justice—Jackson's nomination and confirmation to serve on the Supreme Court, is additional evidence that we have ceased to be a systemically racist nation. But we have a long way to go in erasing the vestiges of our long racist history.

CHAPTER 11

The Unprincipled Media Creates and Exacerbates Divisions

The media no longer reports, with any degree of objectivity or neutrality, about the ideological, partisan, and identity divisions in our broken country. By picking and choosing what to report and how to report it, the advocacy media—which today includes most influential media, ranging from the *New York Times*, to CNN, to Fox, to talk radio, and most social media—<u>create</u> a skewed version of truth in the mind of viewers, readers, and listeners.

Most Americans today pick their media based on what they <u>want</u> the news to be. The last thing they seek is objectivity. Walter Cronkite couldn't get a job in most media today! They want <u>confirmation</u>, rather than <u>information</u> that may lead them to question their biases. They <u>know</u> what their <u>truth</u> is, and they don't want to be confronted with uncertainty, nuance, or cognitive dissonance. They seek comfort in the certainty, not uncomfortable uncertainty. They cheer for reporters who take sides and exaggerate the virtue of their side and the vices of the other side.

Consider Fox host Lara Logan, who claims to have "no agenda." But according to the *Jewish Daily Forward*, she has a "history of anti-Semitism." She has argued that evolution is a Jewish-funded conspiracy to deny God, funded by "the Rothschilds." She repeatedly pushes the incredibly insensitive and historically false analogy between vaccine mandates and the genocide of the Jews during the

Holocaust. She supports the comparison between Dr. Anthony Fauci and Josef Mengele, who used Jewish children for experimentation and then murdered them. Various Jewish organizations, such as the Anti-Defamation League and several Holocaust Museums, condemned "the use" of the Holocaust "to further agendas and causes" unrelated to that unique tragedy and arguing that "these odious comparisons only serve to trivialize and distort the meaning of the Holocaust." In response to these legitimate concerns, Logan retweeted a Tweet from one Jewish supporter:

> Shame on the Auschwitz Museum for slamming Lara Logan for sharing that Jews like me believe that Fauci is a modern day Mengele.

Apparently, as long as the "reporter" is on the "right" side of an issue—in this case critical of vaccination—some people will support anything they say. This is true of both sides of the political spectrum. And it is true not only of political issues, but of racial, gender, and other identity issues as well.

Consider CNN's decision to fire Chris Cuomo for helping his brother deal with sexual harassment charges. The reality is that not a single CNN viewer was misled by Chris Cuomo's activities on behalf of his brother. Everyone knew he was a loyal brother first and that he would put his love for his brother before any commitment to objectivity—as if CNN ever has such a commitment when it comes to politics. Anyone who watched the "Chris-Andy" love fest "interviews" would have expected about as much objectivity as Bobby Kennedy had when he was John Kennedy's attorney general. CNN viewers got exactly what Jeff Zucker, the boss, wanted them to get: an intimate, insider look into the Cuomo brothers and how they were dealing with the governor's problems.

No one was surprised to learn that Chris was helping his brother. To the contrary, they would have been shocked to learn if he wasn't—and they wouldn't have believed any such denials. Viewers aren't as dumb or uncritical as Zucker suggests they are. They see what they see, and they saw the close interaction between the brothers. They would not be surprised to learn that Chris reached out to his media sources or took other actions that a brother would take.

Nor was Zucker misled. He invited the interaction. It boosted ratings for CNN's prime time show when they were plummeting in relation to its competitors. If Zucker were really concerned about objectivity, he could have temporarily suspended his primary anchor for the duration of the investigation. That was his responsibility as the boss to make that decision, not that of the employee to seek a leave. The buck stops with Zucker, who was obviously more interested in making more bucks from his anchor than being Caesar's wife with regard to neutrality.

Moreover, firing Cuomo after his brother left office does nothing to undo any lack of neutrality in his past reporting or to prevent any future lack of objectivity. It is simply punishment for past acts that were mostly known to and validated by Zucker. It is scapegoating and blame shifting for actions that misled no one.

If anyone should have been punished, it is Zucker who has presided over a once objective network that has become under his leadership a biased, one-sided collection of advocates rather than journalists—with some exceptions. It has taken many other actions that willfully mislead millions of viewers and Zucker has blessed if not promoted them. I know, because I am a victim of one such action that was—and still is—much more misleading than anything Chris Cuomo has been accused of: they doctored the recording of my answer during President Trump's first senate impeachment trial to make it appear that I said exactly the opposite of what I actually said. And they refused to correct it, even though the evidence was indisputable and on tape. I am now suing them for misleading their viewers and defaming me. This is only one of several suits CNN has been served with for misleading viewers during the Zucker era; they settled a defamation case against a Catholic High School student who they falsely characterized as a racist. They will be facing other suits as well, perhaps in the Kyle Rittenhouse case.

Zucker and CNN also contributed to the false reporting about the Jussie Smollett case. They, like much of the "woke" media simply couldn't believe that a prominent African American actor, who is both Black and gay would concoct a story about being beaten by Trump supporters. Smollett's story was just too good: it fit perfectly into the progressive narrative about America being a systemically racist and homophobic country. Why then investigate the counter-narrative? So, much of the media simply reported Smollett's allegation as if it were self-proving because of who made it. Identity politics became identity media reporting—and lack thereof.

In that case—unlike with Chris Cuomo—the viewers were in fact mislead. They were also misled by Don Lemon's allegedly "objective" reporting about the Smollett case. In fact, they are close friends and Lemon advised Smollett not to hand his phone to the police. But he did not disclose his role in this case when he discussed it. This was deliberate misleading—and under Zucker's watch—was clearly the responsibility of Zucker and his team. Yet there were no consequences. Nor were there consequences when Lemon was accused of sexual misconduct—which he has vehemently denied and may well be untrue. But when Cuomo complained about his firing, CNN raised the harassment allegations against him—which may also be untrue. This double standard reflects payback rather than principle.

The irresponsibility of the advocacy media—of which CNN has become a prime example—transcends Cuomo, Lemon, me, or any other individuals. It contributes to the ugly divisions our country is experiencing and it understandably reduces the trust we have in the increasingly influential and divisive media.

Zucker recently "resigned" under pressure from CNN for his failure to disclose an affair with a subordinate. It has also experienced a change in ownership that may produce a return to the days when that network was known for its unbiased 24/7 reporting. Such a change, not only by CNN but by other media as well, would help heal the divisive wounds being suffered by our body politic.

Media bias is not limited to this country. Recently, the BBC—Great Britain's national media company—apologized for interviewing me about the Ghislaine Maxwell verdict. That benighted apology raises fundamental questions about the role of the media in reporting on disputed allegations of sexual misconduct. It reflects a widespread refusal by many journalists to fairly report on both sides of the story or to investigate credible claims by the accused that the allegations are false. The fear that if they do, they will be accused of shaming or silencing victims of sexual abuse. I know, because I have provided reporters with incontestable recorded evidence that they promised to publish and failed to report, while reporting on any testimony that bolsters the credibility of alleged victims. The result of this one-sided presentation is to deny the public information necessary to evaluate the comparative credibility of the accusers and the accused, and to encourage false accusations.

Following the conviction of Ghislaine Maxwell, the BBC reached out to me for an interview, as did other media. The media also interviewed several of Maxwell's alleged victims and their supporters, as they have in the past. During the BBC interview and others, I explicitly disclosed that Virginia Giuffre had accused me and others of having sex with her. I did not present myself as a neutral legal expert, but rather as a victim of a false accusation, challenging the credibility of my accuser. I commented that the Maxwell prosecutors were smart not to have called Giuffre as witness because she lacked credibility.

The media, including the BBC, had previously failed to report on why the Maxwell prosecutors had decided not to call Ghislaine Maxwell's most prominent public accuser as a witness against her. This was an important point, especially for British viewers who are obviously interested in Giuffre's accusations and lawsuit against Prince Andrew. Giuffre is Prince Andrew's only accuser and her credibility, or lack thereof, is central to evaluating the accusation. If prosecutors have doubts about the credibility of Prince Andrew's accuser, the British public should be made aware of the basis for those doubts.

They should know, as they were informed by me, that I, too have been accused by Giuffre—along with other high-profile people. So, I told the BBC viewers the truth about why prosecutors decided not to vouch for Giuffre's credibility. No one was misled about my interest in discrediting my false accuser. There was no pushback by the

BBC interviewer, because everything I said was backed with documentary evidence. So why did the BBC apologize for interviewing me? Obviously because of the criticism they received, including from members of their parliament and other politicians.

One such politician, British Labor Party MP Nadia Whittome, demanded that "the BBC should not give a platform to people accused of child sexual abuse," because "we have a responsibility to believe people when they disclose sexual abuse." In other words, even those who have been falsely accused should be silenced and only their accusers, even if the evidence of their mendacity is overwhelming, should be given a platform and believed. The real complaint was not that the BBC failed to alert its viewers of my interest in the case, because I did so.

Those who complained about my interview simply didn't want my point of view to be aired by <u>anyone</u>. This is clear from the complaint directed to the BBC regarding its decision to interview Ian Maxwell, who everyone knows is Ghislaine's brother. The complaint is that defenders of Maxwell shouldn't be given airtime, only the alleged victims should—as they have been, with no complaints.

This is a call for censorship and for only one side of a disputed accusation to be heard. It is precisely this censorial attitude that prevailed during McCarthyism, when people were falsely accused of communist affiliation and were denied airtime to defend themselves. The media refused to report on their side of the story for fear of being accused of victim shaming, even if the alleged victims are themselves victims.

All sides of these important issues should be heard. Alleged victims should not be silenced, nor should those who credibly dispute their allegations. Indeed, real victims can also be perpetrators. Giuffre may well have been victimized by Epstein, but as I explained earlier, another Epstein victim testified at the Maxwell trial that Giuffre victimized her and committed the crime of sex trafficking of minors.

As well, if Giuffre lied under oath about having sex with numerous prominent individuals—as she has about me—she has also committed perjury. All these issues should be fully investigated by the media, as well as by law enforcement. The public has the right to know these sordid details about Giuffre in order to evaluate her allegations against so many prominent people.

There should be no presumption of guilt, as Ms. Whittome proposes. Indeed, what she proposes is more than a mere presumption, it is a certainty assured by the censorship of any opposing views.

I welcome a full and complete investigation by the BBC of their interview with me, as I have called for a full investigation by the FBI of Giuffre's accusations and my documented reproof. I will be happy to present the BBC with the evidence that I have given law enforcement officials in the United States, including Giuffre's own emails and other writings, which prove conclusively that her accusations against me are entirely made up, that I never even met her, and that she collected between $18 and $20 million from her accusations against others. I will also provide them with the recorded statements by her own lawyers acknowledging that Giuffre was wrong. Let not the media silence the falsely accused and let not politicians call for an end to the presumption of innocence.

The BBC has not contacted me as part of its investigation. It has merely investigated the reason why they interviewed me, not whether the interview was appropriate, given that I disclosed my interest as a victim of Giuffre's false allegation.

Perhaps the BBC should have included some of the above facts in their introduction of me. That is on them, but I quickly made up for any such BBC omission myself by clearly stating that I was among those accused by Giuffre. I certainly did nothing wrong by accepting the BBC invitation to be interviewed any more than alleged victims and their supporters did by being interviewed. At the very least, the BBC investigation should conclude that I did nothing improper in being interviewed, instead of implying that I did something unethical.

I will continue to speak out about the false accusations against me, whether on the BBC or other media, especially if the media persists in its refusal to investigate the credibility of those who have made serious, but credibly disputed allegations. No one is trying to silence the alleged victims of sexual abuse like Virginia Giuffre, who has been interviewed by many TV programs, newspapers, magazines, and blogs, and no one should silence those, like me, who seek to prove we are victims of false accusations.

The media and politicians have no right to censor the victims of false charges in the name of political correctness; the public has the right to know the whole truth. I provided an important part of the truth. I was as a suitable person to interview by the media, as are alleged victims and their supporters.

This is yet another example of the widespread problem of the mainstream media taking sides in "reporting" on divisive issues. There is little nuanced or balanced reporting on disputed claims of sexual misconduct, especially, but not exclusively, by women against men. In principle, there should be no presumption in favor or against the accuser or accused. But in our age of identity politics, gender seems to count more than evidence.

CHAPTER 12

The Misuse of Principle by Academics

I f there is one calling that is supposed to be principled rather than
partisan it is academia.

The job of the professor is to teach the student <u>how</u> to <u>think</u>
honestly about complex subjects, not <u>what</u> to <u>believe</u> about controversial issues. It is an abuse of the professor's "academic freedom"
to deny or constrain the academic freedom of his or her students.
Yet in recent years, it has become acceptable among many academics to impose their partisan and ideological beliefs on students who
they grade, recommend, and otherwise influence their careers. This
is especially true in law schools, political science departments, and
"identity politics" departments, such as Black studies, women's studies, gay studies, Middle East politics, Native American studies, and
other such advocacy centers and departments. For example, "critical race theory," "intersectionality" and other such "academic" con-
structs brook no dissent. Anyone "critical" of critical race theory is
regarded as a racist. Professors have been summoned before "diversity committees" and threatened if they are insufficiently committed
to politically correct diversity, equity, and inclusion programs.[1] Yet

---

1   See e.g., Peter Boghassian, "My University Sacrificed Ideas for Ideology. So Today
    I Quit." *Common Sense*, Sep. 8, 2021, available at https://bariweiss.substack.com/p/
    my-university-sacrificed-ideas-for.

studies show that many of these programs, as the people in charge of them, "express anti-Israel attitudes that are so out of proportion and imbalanced as to constitute anti-Semitism."[2] This creates significant problems for Jewish faculty members and students who refuse, on principle, to support programs with which they understandably disagree.

A friend who has been teaching at a major university for decades was recently called before such a committee. He had attended a university sponsored program on "pink washing," which is the anti-Semitic claim that Israel supports gay rights only to deflect from its "bad" human rights record on other issues, particularly with regard to Palestinians. During the question period, my friend politely asked about the record of the Palestinian Authority and Hamas toward gay Arabs. For asking that appropriate and relevant question, my friend was told to leave the meeting, which he did. Several days later he was summoned before a university committee and accused of expressing "anti-Muslim views."

At about the same time, a University of Southern California student who "works as a diversity, equity, and inclusion senator," tweeted: "I want to kill every motherfucking Zionist. Zionists are going to fucking pay. Long live the Intifada. I fucking love Hamas." Yasmeen Mashayekh, who is 21, apparently retained her diversity position because, according to the president and provost, it would be illegal "for the university to remove anyone from a student-elected position based on protected speech."[3]

Does anyone actually believe that the response would be the same if a student senator had made similar threats against Black Lives Matter, gay rights, or pro-Palestinian activities? The double standard is palpable not only in the above examples, but in numerous others in universities around the country. The sad reality is that this unprincipled double standard is not only tolerated by many academics and university administrators, it is created and encouraged by them.

---

2 Jay Greene and James Paul, "Inclusion Delusion: The Anti-Semitism of Diversity Equity and Inclusion Staff at Universities," the Heritage Foundation, Dec. 8, 2021.

3 Ian Spiegelman, "USC In Free Speech Furor Over Student Who Tweeted 'I Want to Kill Every Motherf-cking Zionist'" *Los Angeles* magazine, Dec. 17, 2021.

This lack of principled consistency is most apparent when it comes to race, religion, ethnicity, gender, sexual orientation, and other identity politics. But it is also present along political party lines. Simply put, much of today's academy is dominated by the "progressive" wing of the Democratic Party. Following the election of President Trump, the academy became part of "the resistance." Even lifelong Republicans—few as they were in many universities— joined the resistance. That is, of course, their personal <u>right</u>. What is <u>not</u> their right is to allow their personal political preferences, correct as they may be, to influence their teaching, grading, mentoring, hiring, recommending, or other powers they have over students. They must be fair—to students who disagree with their politics.

They must also be fair and nonpartisan in their scholarship, as distinguished from their public advocacy. This may be a difficult line to draw in close cases, but there are cases which clearly cross any reasonable line. I was involved in one such case, which may be among the worst instance of misusing scholarship for crass partisan purposes.

In my Senate argument against impeaching President Trump, on what I believe were on unconstitutional grounds, I had cited Harvard Law School Assistant Professor Nikolas Bowie (who I don't know) for the proposition that a president can be impeached <u>only</u> for having committed criminal-like behavior, akin to treason or bribery. Bowie had written that a broader interpretation of the impeachment clause is not consistent with the text, spirit, or history of the Constitution.

Critiquing the conversational wisdom of law professors on this issue, Bowie wrote:

> These law professors all may be right about impeachable offenses in a realpolitik sense: only the House and Senate can judge whether President's conduct is truly worthy of impeachment and conviction. But they are wrong to conclude that it is consistent with the text or spirit of the Constitution to convict someone for conduct that was lawful when it was done—that is, to convict someone of "high crimes" without law . . .
>
> But offenses—"Crimes"—should always be defined by laws, not by prosecutors. Many of these law professors avoid this

conclusion by labeling an impeachment proceeding as a civil, not criminal, proceeding, or by arguing that the constitutional prohibitions against ex post facto laws and bills of attainder aren't obstacles if Congress wants to retroactively define conduct as a crime. But these evasive maneuvers are inconsistent with the history of impeachments, the text and structure of the Constitution, and the intuitive understanding that articles of impeachment aren't a recall or a referendum but rather an accusation that the President deserves punishment for past conduct.[4]

Professor Bowie actually went beyond my argument that an impeachable offense must include "criminal-like behavior akin to treason or bribery." He argued that his scholarship supported the view that impeachable conduct must be defined <u>by existing criminal laws</u>— in other words, must be <u>an actual crime,</u> rather than "criminal-like behavior."

But when Bowie learned that I had cited his article in my defense of President Trump, he became upset and decided that he had to distance himself from any defense of Trump based on his scholarship. So he wrote an op-ed in the *New York Times* demanding that his law review article, essentially arguing that impeachment requires that a president committed a crime, should not be used as a defense for this *particular* president. Bowie wrote,

> Mr. Dershowitz apparently thought my article supported his view that even if Mr. Trump did everything the House has accused him of doing, the president shouldn't be convicted because he hasn't been accused of criminal behavior. As an academic, my first reaction was to be grateful that someone had actually read one of my articles. But as a legal academic, my second reaction was confusion. Even if you think impeachment requires a crime, as I do, that belief hardly supports the president's defense or Mr. Dershowitz's position.

---

4   Nikolas Bowie, "High Crimes Without Law," *Harvard Law Review Forum*, p. 63–64.

When interviewed on CNN with Jeffrey Toobin and Anderson Cooper, Bowie engaged in ad hominem attacks, saying that I misconstrued his views and arguing that I made "an irresponsible and ludicrous argument"—when in fact, I made his very own argument using his own scholarly research! I invite everyone to read Bowie's article and judge for themselves whether my reading of his argument was fair. It was.[5] What was unfair, unscholarly, unacademic, and unprincipled was for him to twist and misread his own words for partisan political purposes. Nor is Bowie the only academic to misuse scholarship for partisan purposes.

The most prominent example of the abuse of academic status to serve partisan interests is my former colleague, Professor Laurence Tribe. Tribe used his past credentials as a constitutional scholar to advocate clearly unconstitutional partisan misuses of the impeachment criteria, which are only, "Treason, bribery or other high crimes and misdemeanors." He advocated Trump's impeachment <u>even before</u> Trump took office: "impeachment of Trump should begin on inauguration day." This, despite the absence of any precedent or other legitimate basis for impeaching a president for conduct that took place while he was a private citizen! Nor did Tribe cite any such basis for this extraordinary, unprincipled, and unconstitutional action—except that Professor Tribe, a leading authority on the Constitution, called for it, so it <u>must</u> be constitutional.

These "dia<u>Tribes</u>" continued, with Tribe assuring his students and followers, after Trump was in office for merely one week, that he "must be impeached for abusing his power and shredding the Constitution, <u>more monstrously than any other president in American history</u>."

This deliberate misreading of history by a scholar who claims expertise in American constitutional history is inexcusable. He gave no valid examples of what he claimed was the most monstrous shredding of the Constitution. Nor did he cite other examples of abuse by former presidents, including the genocidal actions of Andrew Jackson

---

5   I argued that Trump was being impeached for non-criminal conduct, i.e., abuse of power and obstruction of Congress, not that Trump <u>could not</u> have been charged with criminal conduct. The House could have, in theory, accused him of criminal conduct, but it chose not to, presumably because a majority concluded that the evidence did not support a criminal charge.

against native Americans; the ending of reconstruction by Andrew Johnson; the racist detention of more than 100,000 Americans of Japanese ethnicity by Franklin Delano Roosevelt; and the crimes and cover-ups of Richard Nixon. If Tribe says Trump's action during his first week in office were worse than those of "any other president" during their full terms in office, it must be so. Because Tribe said it, and he is a constitutional historian who should be trusted.

The only defense that could be made of Tribe's misuse of his academic credentials to serve his partisan interests is that Tribe's overt partisanship is so transparent and obvious that it misleads no one, except those who want to be misled. Consider for example, his change of mind regarding whether a sitting president can be formally charged with a crime allegedly committed while in office, and put on trial in an ordinary criminal court (in addition to, or instead of, being impeached by the House and tried by the Senate). When Bill Clinton was president, Tribe said that he could <u>not</u> be charged with a crime while serving. But when Trump became president, Tribe said a sitting president could be charged and tried and ridiculed those who said he couldn't.[6]

---

6   Tribe has accused me of changing my views as well, but the situation is entirely different. During the impeachment and removal trial of President Bill Clinton back in 1998, I had been interviewed by Larry King. In that interview, I expressed the view that a technical crime was not required for impeachment. I had not researched that issue thoroughly at the time because it was not disputed that Clinton had been charged with a crime, namely perjury. The issue in the Clinton case was whether perjury about a private matter—Clinton's sex life—was a high crime. I said it was a low crime and thus not subject to impeachment. In the King interview, I made an off-the-cuff comment that a technical crime was not required if the impeachment targets a person who "completely corrupts the office of the president, who abuses trust and who poses a great danger to our liberty."

At the time I made it, I was aware that the academic consensus was consistent with the view I then expressed, and so I simply went along with that consensus, without doing my own research about an issue that was not germane to the Clinton case.

In the Trump case, on the other hand, the critical issue was whether a crime was required for impeachment, because the articles of impeachment did not charge any crime. In doing research for my book, *The Case Against Impeaching Trump*, I concluded that the views I expressed in 1998 were not entirely correct. My research convinced me that although a technical crime was not required, as I had said back then, criminal-type behavior akin to treason and bribery was required. More importantly, it was clear that abuse of power or other vague criteria would not be consistent with the words of the Constitution or with the intentions of its Framers.

What changed? Not the words of the Constitution. Not its history. Only the name and party of the White House incumbent. One constitutional rule for Clinton. Another for Trump. That's the "principle" according to Tribe. To paraphrase Groucho Marx, Tribe was essentially saying: These are my principles for Democrats, but if you don't want them applied to Republicans, "well, I have others!"

Tribe's views on what constitutes an impeachable offense under the Constitution also seems to depend on <u>who</u> is president and <u>which</u> party is in power. As Professor Jonathan Turley recounted:

> Tribe in 1998 rejected even criminal bribery and perjury (and possible murder) as impeachable offenses in opposing the impeachment of Bill Clinton. Now [in 2021] however he believes that a tweet can be impeachable if made from the White House, or apparently a campaign finance violation that occurred before inauguration. The tweet is particularly interesting since Tribe stated in 1998 that there must be a certain leeway given to partisan decisions and statements for a president: "letting partisan considerations affect one's decisions, for example, is always an impeachable abuse of power in a judge. Almost never would it be in a President."
>
> In 1998, he opposed impeachment which included an obstruction charge against Clinton, including conduct taken while in office. Now, however, Tribe had advocated both prosecution and impeachment on a myriad of poorly defined obstruction theories despite the failure of Special Counsel Robert Mueller to find evidence of intent to obstruct.[7]

As Professor Turley has also documented, Tribe rarely responds <u>on the merits</u> to contrary views, preferring instead to hurl invectives and level personal attacks:

> In the end, my main objection to Tribe's analysis is not simply his personal or ad hominem attacks. It is the other consistent element:

7   Jonathan Turley, "Impeaching in the Age of Trump: Laurence Tribe's Evolving Views of Impeachable Conduct," available at https://jonathanturley.org/2021/01/29/tribe-in-the-age-of-trump-the-evolving-views-of-impeachable-conduct/

certainty. In the Clinton and Trump impeachments, Tribe regularly claimed clarity and certainty on issues that have divided academics. Appearing on CNN, Trump regularly assures viewer that opposing positions are stupid and nonsensical and personally attacks both political and academic figures. That undermines what is an important debate.[8]

Among Tribe's ad hominem attacks, he has called Professor Turley a "hack," Senator McConnell a "flagrant dickhead," and President Trump "dickhead in chief." He has characterized my constitutional arguments as "idiotic" and "bizarre,"[9] diagnosed me as suffering from

---

8   Ibid.

9   Ironically, the constitutional views I expressed in the Senate in opposition to Trump's impeachment are very close to those expressed by Tribe when he testified against President Clinton's impeachment in 1998:

"Removing a President, even just impeaching him, paralyzes the country. Removing him decapitates a coordinate branch. And remember that the President's limited term provides a kind of check, and if the check fails, he can be prosecuted when he leaves.

To impeach on the novel basis suggested here when we have impeached only one President in our history, and we have lived to see that action universally condemned; and when we have the wisdom not to impeach Presidents Reagan or Bush over Iran-Contra; and when we have come close to impeaching only one other President for the most wide-ranging abuse of presidential power subversive of the Constitution would lower the bar dramatically, would trivialize a vital check. It may be a caged lion, but it will lose its fangs if we use it too promiscuously and would permanently weaken the President and the Nation, leaving a legacy all of us in time would come to regret deeply.

[W]hat the Judiciary Committee does today in attempting to define impeachable offenses will set the stage on which future struggles over the possible impeachment of presidents to come, including presidents yet unborn, will be waged. Indeed, how this Subcommittee and ultimately the House of Representatives (and possibly the Senate) define impeachable offenses in this proceeding will play an important role not only on those occasions, hopefully rare, when the nation again focuses its energies and its attention on the possible impeachment and removal of a sitting president, but in the day-to-day life of the republic, shaped as it is by the strength or weakness of the presidential office, by the relationship between the executive and legislative branches, and by the kinds of people who feel called to public service and are willing to endure its rigors in whatever atmosphere of oversight—from the most positive to the most poisonous—awaits our public servants, including our presidents. For this reason, it would be short-sighted indeed for any witness before this body, or for any member of Congress, to approach the task of defining "high crimes and misdemeanors" from a narrowly result-oriented perspective.

"Dersh-o-mania," and called me a "danger to democracy." He has, however, refused to debate me on the merits of my views or his.

[A]nyone who lowers the bar on what constitutes an impeachable offense simply in an effort to "get" President Clinton, whether for partisan reasons or in a spirit of equally genuine patriotism, may live to regret the abuses by future congresses, and the resulting incapacity of future presidents, that might just as easily be unleashed were we to establish a precedent making it too easy—easier than the Constitution contemplated—to remove a president simply because, as in a parliamentary system, the legislature has come to disagree profoundly with his or her public policies or personal proclivities and has thus lost confidence in the President's leadership.

Not knowing whose ox might be gored in the long run by an error in either direction, anyone who takes the task ahead with the seriousness its nature demands will necessarily proceed under what the philosopher John Rawls famously described as a veil of ignorance that can help us all go forward in a manner sufficiently focused on the long run and insulated against the temptations of short-term rewards and punishments.

Thus, the statements sometimes heard to the effect that an impeachable offense is whatever the House and Senate say is true only in the most cynical and constitutionally faithless sense. If members of this body believe the President should be censured, mechanisms to achieve that end are available. If members believe the President should be criminally prosecuted, that remains an option after he leaves office. [it] would set a horrific precedent—and would punish the entire nation in order to administer punishment to the President. I would urge every member to focus not on what we should do to Bill Clinton but on what impeaching Bill Clinton would do to the country—and to the Constitution.

To raise or to lower the impeachment bar as time goes on is to move the nation closer to an imperial presidency or to a parliamentary system, depending entirely on which way the impeachment winds are blowing. But those are not changes we should make casually or as the accidental byproducts of steps taken for entirely different reasons. If it is a parliamentary system people want, or something closer to such a system than we have had for two centuries, then amending the Constitution to achieve such a system or an approximation thereto is the only constitutionally proper course. Weakening the presidency through watering down the basic meaning of "high Crimes and Misdemeanors" seems a singularly ill-conceived, even a somnambulistic, way of backing into a new—and, for us at least, untested—form of government."

Excerpts from Laurence Tribe's Testimony in the Impeachment of President William Jefferson Clinton, Hearing of the Subcommittee on the Constitution— "Background and History of Impeachment" (November 9, 1998), Ser. No. 63, p. 218 ff

Tribe made precisely the opposite "constitutional" arguments after Trump was elected! On the other hand, I presented essentially the same arguments against the impeachment of Clinton and Trump.

Imagine how a student who held views similar to those characterized by Tribe as "idiotic" would feel expressing such views in class or on an exam?[10] Or imagine how a law student might feel if his constitutional law professor urged his university to take steps to evade a Supreme Court decision as some pro-segregation lawyers did following the 1954 Supreme Court decision in *Brown v. Board of Education* mandating the end of public school segregation. They proposed ways by which the schools could deal with that decision without radically altering the actual composition of segregated schools. They cautioned, however, that the school boards would have to be "more subtle" than they have been thus far, lest they be caught violating the decision.

I was reminded of that despicable effort to circumvent that important Supreme Court decision by a statement recently made by Professor Tribe. He told the *Harvard Crimson* that he remains confident in Harvard's ability to adapt its admissions process without decreasing the number of minority students should the court strike down race-based affirmative action.

His exact words, which I now quote, are strikingly parallel to those used by southern segregationists eager to maintain the then status quo: "Universities as intelligent as Harvard will find ways of dealing with the decision without radically altering their composition," Tribe said. "But they will have to be more subtle than they have been thus far."

There is a difference between *predicting* that universities may try to circumvent a decision, and *advising* universities to be "more subtle" in doing so. Tribe has crossed that line.

---

10 Contrast this with student reviews given to now-Justice Brett Kavanaugh when he was visiting professor at Harvard Law School. The *New York Times* reported that students would praise Kavanaugh's evenhandedness, quoting one student as having said, "While most of the class shared rather conservative views," the student wrote, "the judge presented the other side quite well, even though he likely shared most of those conservative views." The student added that "many of the HLS professors could learn from his acceptance of views across the political spectrum." Adam Liptak, "'Best Professor.' 'Very Evenhanded.' 'Great Hair!': Brett Kavanaugh, as Seen by His Law Students," *New York Times*, July 19, 2018.

This legal advice from a Harvard professor, who purports to be an expert in Constitutional law, essentially suggests that Harvard engage in conduct similar to that rightfully condemned when engaged in by southern school boards in an effort to circumvent *Brown v. Board of Education.*

Supporters of Tribe will obviously try to distinguish the two cases: Brown was a good case; a decision outlawing race-based affirmative action would be a bad case. But lawyers should not ethically recommend circumventing Supreme Court decisions based on whether they regard them as good or bad. A precedent set in bad cases will inevitably be employed to circumvent good cases.

That is precisely what Texas is trying to do in dealing with *Roe v. Wade*, by authorizing vigilante plaintiffs to sue abortion providers. Constitutional law professors should not be advising their universities to use "subtle" means to circumvent Supreme Court decisions, even if they disagree with them.

It would be perfectly proper for Tribe and others to recommend proper ways of dealing with an adverse Supreme Court decision. These may include legislation, administrative actions, petitions for rehearing, constitutional amendments—and even court packing (though I strongly disagree with that tactic). But it does not include using subtle means to deliberately circumvent a Supreme Court ruling.

Professor Tribe is well known for his view that good ends justify bad means. For Tribe, the Constitution means what he thinks it means. He approves of race-based affirmative action, and so it is perfectly proper for universities to engage in subtle efforts to evade a decision striking down a policy of which Tribe approves.

This is not the way the Constitution should work. Every action should pass what I call the "shoe on the other foot test." No tactic should be recommended for one side that would not be proper if used by the other side.

It is far from certain that the Supreme Court will outright ban all race-based affirmative action programs. The vote is too close to call. But if it does, the proper response is not to circumvent it. There are alternatives to race-based admissions that actually would be fairer and more consistent with the equal protection clause of the Constitution. These include a focus on individual applicants, based on their personal experiences, rather than on racial categories.

For example, Justice William O. Douglas—perhaps the most liberal person ever to serve on the Supreme Court—recommended race-neutral admissions policies that would not prefer a wealthy Black applicant over "a poor Appalachian white or a second-generation Chinese [American] in San Francisco, or some other American whose lineage is too diverse as to defy ethnic labels."

The end result of such a color blind admissions policy would be to reduce the number of privileged Black applicants, while increasing the number of underprivileged Black and non-Black applicants. This would not be a circumvention of the Supreme Court decision outlining race-based affirmative action programs. It would be the implementation of a more complex and more difficult to administer admissions process that would also be more consistent with the Constitution.

But in the age of identity politics—where race seems to matter more than individual characteristics—universities might well seek ways around the anticipated Supreme Court decision. They will turn to constitutional lawyers like Tribe to assist them in this dangerous and ethically questionable endeavor. The end result would not be good for anyone.

Tribe's most recent attempt to distort the Constitution into a defense of his partisan views came when he accused Tucker Carlson and Fox News of "treason, as defined by Article III of the US Constitution," for "throwing its weight behind Putin." Both Tribe and I opposed US policy in the Vietnam War, in invading Iraq, and in other military adventures. According to Tribe's willfully distorted view of the Constitution, we too, would be guilty of treason for giving "aid and comfort to an enemy." The First Amendment be damned if it suits Tribe's partisan views. The right to protest our foreign policy extends only to foreign policies which Tribe opposes, not those with which he agrees.

After receiving much criticism for his absurd views of the treason and speech provisions of the Constitution, Tribe took down his laughable tweet and put up one that totally mischaracterized what he originally tweeted, accusing his critics of thinking that "I meant to be using the word 'treason' literally." Duh! Tribe had originally tweeted that Carlson and Fox would appear to be guilty of treason "as defined by Article III." What could be more literal than that!

As further proof of Tribe's misuse of his "expertise" on the Constitution, consider what he tweeted during the dispute over the counting of the electoral vote in 2021. He accused members of Congress who objected to the vote count of crossing the "line past sedition [to] domestic terrorism and treason."

Tribe may be the most extreme example of an unprincipled partisan using his academic credentials as a political weapon, but he is not the only one.

On the eve of the second impeachment trial of former President Trump, more than 140 constitutional scholars issued a public threat to his lawyers demanding, in effect, that they not make arguments to the Senate regarding the First Amendment. This unreasonable threat came in the form of a claim that "any First Amendment defense" raised by the attorneys for Trump "would be legally frivolous."

This threat is dangerous to our adversary system of justice and wrong as a matter of constitutional law. It is dangerous since the rules of professional responsibility prohibit an attorney from making frivolous arguments and carry disciplinary sanctions for anyone who does it. The letter purports to put these lawyers on notice that if they offer any kind of First Amendment defense, they subject themselves to potential discipline.

The argument is also wrong on its merits as a matter of constitutional law, as I have demonstrated.[11] However, the most dangerous aspect of the letter is that its goal is to chill the lawyers for Trump from making some important arguments on behalf of their client. The letter easily could have said that any First Amendment argument would be wrong, but instead it goes further and suggests that any such argument is prohibited in the code of professional responsibility for attorneys and could result in disciplinary sanctions.

---

11 *The Hill*, Feb. 8, 2021. See also, *Inside Higher Education*, Feb. 14, 2020.

As a professor of legal ethics for more than two decades at Harvard Law School, I can assure Trump's lawyers that these scholars are wrong.[12] Arguments to the Senate based on the First Amendment are not frivolous. They should be offered vigorously and responsibly without fear of ethical ramifications. What is of dubious ethics is for these scholars to try to frighten lawyers away from making plausible arguments with a threat that they will face sanctions for it. I offered to support any attorney who makes responsible First Amendment arguments to the Senate and is disciplined.

As a constitutional lawyer who has litigated some of the most important First Amendment cases in the last half century, including those involving the Pentagon Papers, the film *I Am Curious Yellow*, the Broadway production of *Hair*, the Chicago Seven protesters, CIA analyst Frank Snepp, adult film star Harry Reems, and the WikiLeaks case, I stand relatively confident the current Supreme Court would find the ill-advised and justly condemnable speech by Trump on January 6, 2021 to be fully protected under the Brandenburg principle, which distinguishes between advocacy and incitement to violence. Trump used provocative words, however, they included the plea for his listeners to protest "peacefully and patriotically." Further, he never outright urged violence or lawlessness.

Compared to the speech in 1964 by Clarence Brandenburg, the neo-Nazi Klansman surrounded by armed men with crosses, the speech by Trump was pablum. It was typical of rousing speeches made over decades by radicals, suffragettes, union leaders, and many others in Washington. It was far less incendiary than the remarks of the Chicago Seven and other activists during the Democratic National Convention of 1968.

Not only would the Supreme Court of today conclude that the speech by Trump was protected advocacy, so would have previous Supreme Courts during the golden age of the First Amendment, which extended from the early 1960s to the start of the 21st century.

---

12 I was not one of Trump's lawyers during the second impeachment, because I did not want to be associated with any claim that the 2020 presidential election was invalid.

Justices Oliver Holmes, Louis Brandeis, Robert Jackson, and other great justices also would have likely found this speech to be well within those protections of the First Amendment.

The letter written by the scholars concedes that only some of its signers agree with its conclusion about the speech as outside the protections of the Supreme Court ruling in Brandenburg. So how could it be frivolous of lawyers for Trump to offer such arguments? The letter contends the First Amendment "simply does not apply" to an impeachment.

This claim flies clearly in the face of the First Amendment, which prohibits Congress from making any law abridging freedom of speech. The federal courts have interpreted that to include any state action, whether in the form of a law or other sanction. It would be one thing if this letter merely said such arguments were wrong. But to declare, as the letter does, the arguments would be frivolous is dangerous and unethical.

The letter also states that "no reasonable scholar or jurist" would make these First Amendment arguments. This sends a chilling message to all current and future law professors that if you desire to be considered "a reasonable scholar or jurist" by your colleagues and by university hiring committees, you will not dare make such constitutional arguments. It also threatens the academic freedom of students to make such argument. I for one continued to make them. I challenged any of the signers to debate me on whether my arguments are reasonable or frivolous. None accepted. Intimidating lawyers, professors, and students from making these important arguments by declaring them frivolous and unreasonable is a form of censorship that is obviously inconsistent with the spirit of our constitutional system. But for many academics "getting" Trump was more important than the principles underlying the First Amendment, academic freedom, and the right to counsel.

Sometimes it takes an absurd event to illustrate the high cost of upholding crucial principles, such as the right to counsel. In making that career choice, I knew that I would be criticized by those who do not understand the constitutional right to counsel and the need for every defendant to receive zealous representation.

But when law professors such as Cornell University's Michael Dorf—who is an acolyte, water carrier, and coauthor of America's most prominent constitutional hypocrite, Professor Laurence Tribe—sets out to defame me, or anyone, for a principled representation of unpopular defendants, it becomes clear, and alarming, how much trouble the Constitution is in. Dorf conducted what he called a "Highly Unscientific Twitter Poll for Most Embarrassing Yale Law School Alum." He put my name prominently on the list because "Dershowitz seems to take special pride in defending people whose alleged conduct he claims to disapprove—including, especially, Donald Trump." Dorf apparently does not remember the principle often attributed to Voltaire: "I disapprove of what you say, but I will defend to the death your right to say it." Dorf acknowledges that some people might dislike me or others because "they disagree with his extreme conception of the lawyer as a zealous advocate."

Dorf also accused me of a willingness "to say fairly outrageous things simply so people pay attention," but without citing a single example from my writings or statements. He could, of course, have cited examples of "outrageous things" from his mentor, Tribe, who garnered media attention by calling Senator Mitch McConnell a "flagrant dickhead" and then-President Donald J. Trump "dickhead-in-chief."

Dorf goes on speciously to say that I deserve special condemnation because I "represent men who behaved terribly towards women (e.g., Claus von Bülow, O. J. Simpson, Mike Tyson, Jeffrey Epstein, Donald Trump) that suggests at least a possibility of misogyny." (In his apparent ignorance and malice, he could not resist the temptation to make a gratuitous reference to the fact I once received a massage in Jeffrey Epstein's home, years before I represented Epstein, but omitting the facts that it was a neck and shoulder massage, that my wife also received a massage administered by a professional therapist who specialized in deep tissue massages, and that I never even met the woman who falsely accused me of having sex with her years after that therapeutic massage.)

In purporting to describe my "career-long oeuvre, a tendency to represent men," Dorf also maliciously omits the fact that I have defended more women than most other criminal lawyers, including Mia Farrow, Patricia Hearst, Leona Helmsley, Gigi Jordan, Lucille Miller, Sandra Murphy, and numerous less well-known women who alleged harassment by men. He also deliberately omits the fact that my "oeuvre" includes representing half of my clients on a pro bono basis and that many of my cases have focused on the First Amendment, the Fourth Amendment, and the death penalty. In light of Dorf's deliberate misrepresentation of my "oeuvre," it is not surprising that I came out ahead of Justice Samuel Alito and even Stuart Rhodes (the founder of "Oath Keepers") in his slanted, left-wing unpopularity poll.

Normally, one would ignore such a childish and malicious enterprise, because the reader is given no idea even of how many people were included in this admittedly "unscientific poll," or how they were selected. He acknowledges that the poll was "lawyer-skewed" and "liberal-skewed," but the fact that so many highly educated people are prepared to condemn a lawyer for his "oeuvre" tells us something chilling about today's legal education that cannot be ignored.

So, I will take my victory in Dorf's dishonor roll as a red badge of courage and continue to represent people whom he and his readers despise. I am proud to have gone to Yale Law School and to be living a life of principle based on what I was taught there by professors such as Alex Bickel, Telford Taylor, Joseph and Abe Goldstein, Jay Katz, and Guido Calabresi. I do not think they would be embarrassed by my "oeuvre." They understood the crucial role of a "zealous lawyer" in our adversary system of justice, even if Dorf and his ilk do not. More importantly, they understood the alternative system that prevails in so many tyrannies, where zealous advocates and their unpopular clients are treated much worse than finishing atop an "unpopularity poll" by an unprincipled partisan like Dorf.

In today's academy, principle too often takes a back seat to partisanship, identity politics, and other left-wing ideologies. This threatens the role of the academy as a politically neutral and principled institution whose goal is the never-ending and honest quest for truth.

CHAPTER 13

The Implications of Punishing Principle and Rewarding Partisan Hypocrisy: Can We Ever Reverse It?

The moralist François Duc de La Rochefoucauld once observed that "hypocrisy is the tribute that vice pays to virtue." That may have been true in an age when virtue was rewarded, and vice punished (if there ever was such an age). It is far less true today, when principled virtue is punished if it does not favor the chosen side, and unprincipled vice is rewarded if it does. Today hypocrisy needs no excuse. It <u>is</u> virtue if it achieves the desired end. Politicians no longer have to deny hypocrisy: Republican leaders defended their decision to confirm Justice Barrett while denying a hearing to Judge Garland merely by asserting their power to do so. When I asked one Republican acquaintance how they could be so hypocritical, he responded with a rhetorical question: "Why do dogs lick their testicles?" He provided the answer to both his and my question: "Because they can."

The Republicans could confirm Gorsuch, and the Democrats could impeach Trump—"because they can." They have the political power, if not the moral and constitutional authority. Partisanship prevails over principle, because "we can" and because "They started it." "We're right, they're wrong," so anything goes.

The demise of principle as a constraint on the exercise of raw political power poses a fundamental danger to our constitutional structure. The Framers constructed a system of institutional checks and balances because they understood that men and women are not angels. As Madison put it: "If men were angels no government would be necessary . . . neither external nor internal controls on government would be necessary." The founders had experienced the hypocrisy that allowed Jefferson to write that "All men are created equal" on a desk brought to him by his very unequal slave. They recognized the need for compromise between principle and pragmatism that enabled them to construct a United States comprised of sovereignties with different values and laws. But principle was always a factor in these compromises. The debates during the constitutional convention and in the advocacy that followed in the Federalist Papers were governed by principle. No one said: We will do it <u>because we can</u>. Hypocrisy was present but it did pay homage to virtue.

In high school we learned that "checks and balances" referred to the three branches of government. But experience has taught us that to work effectively as a check on excesses, these governmental institutions must themselves be checked and balanced by non-governmental sources of power, such as the media, religion, academia, business, and other influencers. Among the most important checks on power is principle. A citizenry that rewards leaders who act on principle and punishes those who do not, serves as a democratic check against the excesses of raw power. A citizenry that has become inured to unprincipled decision-making provides far less of a balance. So, the sacrifice of principle to partisanship has deeper implications than today's headlines. It bodes ill for all Americans who love liberty and despise tyranny, regardless of party affiliation, racial identity, or ideology.

The question remains: Can we restore principle to its proper role in regulating power and partisanship in governance?

In 2004, I wrote a book entitled *Rights from Wrongs: A Secular Theory of the Origin of Rights*. Its thesis is that most of our rights arise out of our collective recognition of injustices—of wrongs. Slavery, gender discrimination, genocide, and other societal wrongs led to an understanding that we need rights to prevent recurrences of these evils. Slavery led to the 13th, 14th, and 15th Amendments and the Civil Rights Movement. Gender discrimination let to the 19th Amendment and gender-equality legislation. The Holocaust led to the Declaration of Human Rights. And so on.

Sometimes the reactions to wrongs produce their own wrongs. The pendulum of justice swings widely and erratically, but I believe American history gives us a cause for cautious optimism. We are a centrist people, subject to occasional extremes on both sides. But these extremes tend to be situational and temporary, though sometimes of considerable duration.

We are now in the midst of a significant reaction—perhaps overreaction—to the Trump presidency and postpresidential antics; to the killing of George Floyd and other racially wrought events; to the exposure of the sexual misconduct of celebrities and other well-known people such as Bill Cosby, Jeffrey Epstein, and Harvey Weinstein; to COVID and the often partisan reactions to it; and to other provocations.

We may soon see a counterreraction to the resulting "reckonings," "cancellations," deprivations of due process, curtailing of free speech, over-emphasis on race and identity politics, responses to COVID, and other current reactions to past wrongs, evils, and dangers.

The future of rights and of principle—which is a close cousin of rights—is uncertain. Although history gives us cause to be cautiously optimistic, demography gives us cause to be cautiously pessimistic, or at least concerned. The current attack on rights, principles, and process comes primarily from young people, who are our future.[1] Many of them are well motivated. They want to end racism, sexism, homophobia, environmental pollution, and other evils. Many of us

---

1   See Jonathan Rauch and Peter Wehner, "What's Happening on the Left Is No Excuse for What's Happening on the Right." *New York Times*, Jan. 22, 2022. https://www.nytimes.com/2022/01/20/opinion/illiberalism-left-right.html (This excellent and balanced analysis omits one critical factor: The oppression by the hard left is generally imposed by young, university educated people who are our future. The hard right is largely our older, less educated past.)

older folk share these goals but worry about the means that radicals seek to employ. I remember how opposed so many in my generation were when conservative Republican presidential candidate Barry Goldwater said: "Extremism in the defense of justice is no vice [and] moderation in the pursuit of justice is no virtue." That has now become the mantra of the radical left. But youth and good motives do not justify bad means. As Justice Louis Brandies warned a century ago: "The greatest dangers to liberty lurk in insidious encroachment by men [and may I add, women] of zeal, well-meaning but without understanding."

Conclusion

Trying to live a principled life—putting principle before political, ideological, or identity preferences—is admirable and should be encouraged. But not all principles are equally praiseworthy. Some of the worst things human beings have done to each other have been justified in the name of some perverse "principle." When I taught a Harvard College freshman seminar on "Where does your morality come from," I assigned 19th-century readings seeking to justify slavery on Christian "principles." I assigned Dostoevsky's "principled" justification for anti-Semitism, and the Supreme Court's "principled" decision denying women the right to practice law rather than raise children. I made "principled" devil's, advocate arguments in favor of capital punishment and torture, which I personally oppose.[1] I assigned legal briefs that offered "principled" constitutional arguments against abortion and gay rights, which I favor. Principle, like scripture, can be cited by the devil.

I challenged the students to ask hard questions about their own moral principles: What are their sources? What makes them better than other principles? Are they subject to exceptions? Under what

---

1   Alan Dershowitz, "The Torture Warrant: A Response to Professor Strauss," *New York Law School Law Review*, Vol. 48, p.275.

circumstances? Are principles really different than strongly held preferences? If so, why should a principle be preferred over a preference? What if equally persuasive principles clash with each other, as many believe they do in the abortion context? How does a principled person choose? Which institutions get to resolve such conflicts in a democratic, three-branch, federal system? Is acting on principle possible or desirable when trying to achieve good ends in a non-principled arena? Is it like bringing a Bible to a gun fight? Martin Luther King thought that the Bible and its principles would win over guns.

Adherence to principles promotes consistency of action, but some believe, with Emerson, that consistency is "the hobgoblin of little minds." The entire quote is a bit more nuanced: "A <u>foolish</u> consistency is the hobgoblin of little minds, adored by little statesmen and philosophers and divines." Emerson offers no alternative to foolish consistency other than wise consistency or situational inconsistency. Is ad hoc decision making with no effort at consistency any less of a hobgoblin?

What distinguishes a <u>foolish</u> consistency from a <u>wise</u> one is the eternal question posed by any system of thought. The answer I offer in this short book is <u>principle</u>. Principled consistency—passing the shoe on the other foot test—is a check on power, especially if the principles themselves are commendable.

I make no claim that adherence to principles will always assure good outcomes—only that principles matter and that there should be a strong presumption in favor of principle when it clashes with partisanship. Such a presumption would be a considerable improvement over today's simple-minded partisan hypocrisy. To paraphrase Churchill: Adherence to principle may be the worst guide to action, except for all the others that have been tried over time.

I end this book with a personal note about the price I have paid and imposed on my family for my commitment—some would say my stubborn commitment—to my principles and my refusal to pick sides in what has become a political and cultural war. A well-meaning friend from Martha's Vineyard who tried hard to persuade me to prioritize my personal needs over my principles put it this way: "The simple solution might have been to follow your good friends and family's advice and kept quiet, and none of what's happened [to you] would have. That was my advice to you five years ago and up until the night before you went to Washington [to argue against Trump's impeachment]. Your world was full and rich with family, friend and yes, a real community that loved and revered you. You were king."

But silence in the face of unprincipled and unconstitutional actions has never been an option for me. My well-intentioned friend did not know me. That's not who I am or have ever been. I deeply regret the pain this has caused members of my family. One of them told me, more in sadness than in anger, that the name Dershowitz used to be a source of pride among their friends and now it is a source of shame—at least for some. A few have lost jobs and other opportunities because they were related to "Trump's lawyer." Most understand me. Some don't.

I have lost friends and acquaintances. A number of "friends" and even relatives who used to benefit from their association with me when I was "king" suddenly began to join the cancel crowd, when they no longer reaped any benefit from their association with a now dethroned "pariah" (at least to some). I learned who my fair-weather "friends" were. In addition to losing some friends, I lost clients, speaking opportunities, honors, and status. Some of this was expected. Some not.

The price of principle is high. I am paying that price. I ask no one to feel sorry for me. I chose my way of life. But the punishments for principle—and the rewards for unprincipled partisanship—transcend me and my family. They reflect a corrosive societal trend that endangers the cohesion of our nation under the rule of law. I will continue to fight for principle, no matter how high the personal price.